THE RUSSIAN NOVEL IN
ENGLISH FICTION

HUTCHINSON'S UNIVERSITY LIBRARY

ENGLISH LITERATURE

EDITOR
PROFESSOR BASIL WILLEY
M.A., F.B.A., HON.LITT.D.
*King Edward VII Professor of English Literature in the
University of Cambridge*

THE RUSSIAN NOVEL
IN ENGLISH FICTION

by

GILBERT PHELPS
M.A.

FORMERLY STRATHCONA RESEARCH STUDENT
AND ASSISTANT SUPERVISOR IN ENGLISH STUDIES,
ST. JOHN'S COLLEGE, CAMBRIDGE

LONDON
HUTCHINSON'S UNIVERSITY LIBRARY

Republished 1971
Scholarly Press, Inc., 22929 Industrial Drive East
St. Clair Shores, Michigan 48080

Hutchinson & Co. (Publishers) Ltd.

178-202 Great Portland Street, London, W.1

London   Melbourne   Sydney   Auckland
Bombay   Johannesburg   New York   Toronto

First published 1956

Library of Congress Catalog Card Number: 79-158907
ISBN 0-403-01301-1

TO

MY MOTHER AND FATHER

CONTENTS

7

PREFACE

I MUST begin by explaining that this book is *not* a history of the Russian Novel: it is a study of the Russian Novel *in English translation*, which is a very different matter. Readers who seek information about Russian literary history, or about the work of individual Russian writers, must turn as I have done to the specialists.

My aim has been to trace the main outlines of the story of the reception of the Russian Novel in England, and to some extent in America, and of its impact upon some of the English and American writers who welcomed it. This story, in my opinion, constitutes a most interesting chapter in the history of the evolution of the English Novel during the nineteenth and early twentieth centuries. It is, however, a large subject which cannot be fully explored in a book of this length. I decided therefore to concentrate on the earlier phases and in particular upon the rôle of Ivan Sergeyevich Turgenev, even though this involved an unsatisfactorily sketchy treatment of the parts played by his great contemporaries and juniors. One of the main justifications for this decision is that these early aspects are perhaps the least known, though the reader will find that other reasons also emerge in the course of my argument. My hope is that I shall be able to redress the balance later in a separate study devoted to the impact of Tolstoy, Dostoyevsky, Chekhov and Gorky.

I also decided to omit discussion of post-revolutionary Russian fiction (apart from one or two references to some of the later work of Gorky) as lying outside the scope of my inquiry, chiefly because English translations of Soviet novelists have so far been comparatively few in number and limited in appeal. I realize, however, that this too is a branch of the subject that demands further study.

In the spelling of Russian names I have followed the system of transliteration employed by D. S. Mirsky in his *History of*

9

Russian Literature (Routledge & Kegan Paul Ltd., 1949), except that for the convenience of the reader I have omitted the accents (unsatisfactory though I know this to be from the point of view of the pronunciation). In quoting, however, I have kept to the forms used by the writer concerned, and for the names of fictional characters I have adopted the forms used in the best known translations.

For the titles of Russian works I have also turned to the most familiar translations—those of Constance Garnett, for example, in the cases of Turgenev, Dostoyevsky, and Chekhov, and those of Louise and Aylmer Maude in the case of Tolstoy, though I am aware that more recent translations may, in some cases, be more reliable. Occasionally I have used a different title, for reasons which are apparent in the text : for example I have preferred *A Nest of Gentlefolk* to Constance Garnett's *A House of Gentlefolk*, because this novel of Turgenev's first became known to English readers in this form, because the title of the French version, which many Englishmen read, was *Une Nichée de Gentilshommes*, and because in any case it is closer to the original. In dealing with specific versions I have of course used the translators' titles.

The dates of Russian writers are given as they occur in the text, but initials are usually omitted. These however will be found against each author's name in the Index.

I have, of course, consulted the various learned dissertations connected with my theme, and the titles of the most important will be found in the Reading List at the end of this book. Other relevant sources of information are indicated in the text.

Some of this material has appeared in the *Cambridge Journal*, the *Cambridge Review*, *Britain To-day*, and in Russia during the war in the *British Ally*. I have also drawn upon a series of scripts which I wrote for the East European Service of the BBC in 1946–47.

I first began studying this subject as a Strathcona Research Student at St. John's College, Cambridge, and I should like to take this opportunity of expressing my thanks to the Master and Fellows. I should also like to thank Professor Basil Willey for persuading me to return to it, and for his help and encouragement in the writing of this book.

GILBERT PHELPS.

December 1955.

CHAPTER ONE

INTRODUCTORY : RENAISSANCE OR FEVER ?

THE works of the great Russian novelists of the nineteenth and early twentieth centuries are now European classics, subject like all classics to the ebb and flow of critical appreciation. The publication during the last few years of important biographies and memoirs and of excellent new translations suggests that at the moment perhaps there is a modest revival of interest. But "the Russian fever" is over, and it is difficult to believe that it once raged so fiercely. It is difficult too, when we look at the novels now being written, to avoid asking ourselves whether the Russian influence was really one of major importance—"the great vivifying current in the sea of modern letters" to quote John Galsworthy—or whether it was merely a passing symptom.

Certainly Mr. Middleton Murry did not feel he was guilty of exaggeration when in 1912 he compared Constance Garnett's translation of *The Brothers Karamazov* with "the most epoch-making translations of the past" and put it on a level with North's *Plutarch*, and neither did the reviewer in the *Spectator* who wrote that "the same vast and potent inspiration which filled so erratically and yet so gloriously the old poets of Renaissance England, still seems to breathe and burn through the novels of modern Russia".

The testimonies of creative writers too could hardly have been more outspoken. There were few, at any rate from 1912 onwards, who did not point to the Russian Novel as one of the most stimulating elements in the cultural atmosphere, and their attitude is summed up by Virginia Woolf's pronouncement in "Modern Fiction" (*The Common Reader*, first series, 1925): "The most elementary remarks upon modern English fiction can hardly avoid some mention of the Russian influence, and if the Russians are mentioned one runs the risk of feeling that to write of any fiction save theirs is a waste of time."

And yet when one looks back over the volume of comment,

a curious fact emerges: that however enthusiastic it may be, it rarely goes beyond the vaguest of generalizations. When we think of the mass of scholarly and critical study devoted to the impact of other foreign literatures, sometimes within quite narrow limits—the influence of the French Symbolists, for example, or even that of individual foreign writers such as Ibsen—it seems surprising that literary historians and critics should have devoted so little space, by comparison, to a phenomenon which some of them had no hesitation in calling a Renaissance.

Never in fact has a major literary influence (if it is that) received such sketchy treatment. When Mr. Gerald Gould in *The English Novel of To-Day* (1924) whets our appetite by heading one of his sections "The Neo-Russians" to denote, he tells us, a whole group of novelists affected by a literary "Russian revolution", and then goes on to tell us that he has not the slightest idea as to which members of this group had studied which of the Russians in particular, or whether indeed they had studied them at all, though he is still sure that there is "an influence, an emanation, an inspiration", we are only encountering an extreme example of the kind of frustration that we come to expect. There can be no doubt in fact that of all literary influences that of the Russian Novel is the least articulated and the most amorphous.

The simple fact of translation is undoubtedly one of the major reasons. Of all the foreign influences that have entered into our literary heritage none has been so completely dependent upon it. Not only the public who read the great Russian novels but also the critics who commented upon them were, for the most part, utterly ignorant of the originals. In addition most of the early translations were clumsy or inaccurate, often indeed at second hand from the French, or even at third hand from the German by way of French versions, and indeed by the time they emerged into English many of them were so bad that those who could do so preferred to trust themselves to the French.

There was no North, or Florio or Munday in fact to serve the great Russian writers, and it was not until the advent of Constance Garnett and Aylmer Maude that the public had the opportunity of reading their complete works in really good English. By then various contortions and oddities of expression had contributed to the Russian atmosphere vibrations and mystifications that were quite extraneous.

The remoteness of the language which the Elizabethan traveller Jerome Horsey had described as "the most copius and elegant . . . in the world", and the distorting mirror in which the early translators reflected it, therefore, accounts in large part for the blurred outlines of the Russian influence. But the confused and excitable background of political and commercial rivalries was at least equally responsible. High temperatures in relation to Russia and things Russian were common long before the "intelligentzia" of the early twentieth century caught the Russian fever. Throughout nearly the whole of the nineteenth century Russia was the bogey man of Europe. The various preconceptions, prejudices, and emotional stereotypes involved, constituted the most unfavourable atmosphere imaginable for peaceful and orderly cultural penetration, and in fact nearly every separate burst of interest in the Russian Novel was directly related to some shift or other in the pattern of Anglo-Russian rivalries and fears.

The change from hatred and suspicion to uneasy alliance, moreover, did not really alter the position, for the Russian Soul was the natural successor to the Russian Bear, and the emotions involved were equally unbalanced. When for example in 1915 Miss Rebecca West wrote :

"We have arrived at intimacy with a people extraordinarily like the English, in their untidiness and their inflexible conviction that there are other things in the world besides efficiency, but sweeter in their hearts, beautifully devoid of the sense of property and beautifully troubled by consciences that are sharp-edged like a child's",

she was merely reversing the coin of the Elizabethan George Turberville's : "A people passing rude, to vices vile inclind."

During this period certainly there could be no doubt of the existence of a Russian influence. As Mr. Somerset Maugham's Ashenden remarks—"it seized upon Europe with the virulence of an influenza epidemic". But though many other factors were involved, the "Russian fever" must also be regarded as one of the more hectic manifestations of war hysteria, and of the equally distorted mood of depression and disillusionment that succeeded it.

In the whole history of the Russian Novel in England therefore it is difficult to point to a single lucid interval in which the normal processes of cultural assimilation and assessment could take place. Fevers, moreover, die down as suddenly as they come, and in the convalescent period the patient, as he looks back upon the course of his illness, tends to wonder whether everything that happened during it was pure hallucination. It was not surprising therefore that when writers and critics began to take stock, after the most hectic symptoms had disappeared, they felt there was little that was tangible for them to lay hold of. The position was in fact summed up perfectly by *The Times Literary Supplement* in 1930, when it decided that it was "not perhaps a strictly definable legacy; it was something in the air, a layer of the atmosphere".

This is a far cry from a "Renaissance". That indeed may have been an extravagant term to apply to what was after all only one of the innumerable threads in the complex pattern of modern thought and feeling—a pattern, moreover, that belonged to a period of flux and dissolution rather than to one that was a "new beginning". It would be possible, too, to argue that the Russian Novel was itself a dissolvent, contributing to a form of Realism that by breaking old moulds and traditions culminated in the dead-end of *Ulysses*. The contemporary novel, it is true, appears to be turning back to earlier traditions, rather than attempting to explore the kinds of themes and experiences with which the great Russian novelists, and if it comes to that most of the great novelists of the period, were concerned. But though it may be true, as Virginia Woolf pointed out in "The Russian Point of View" (*The Common Reader*, first series, 1925), that in the last resort it is "not the samovar but the teapot that rules in England", in a period of reaction writers and critics tend to throw out the baby with the bath water, and the time may have come for us to ask whether there has been any real strengthening of the English tradition, or whether some of the teapots are not being used for the pouring of very small beer. Perhaps in the long run it will be found that "something in the air, a layer of the atmosphere" points in fact to the kind of influence that is the most pervasive and penetrating of all, so that though it may elude the obvious classifications of the historians, and though it may be temporarily ignored, it may still have educated and modified the sensibility of our times. If it was not anything as grandiose as a Renaissance in fact, neither may it have been as evanescent as a fever.

Now the starting-point of the fever was undoubtedly the publication in 1912 of Constance Garnett's translation of *The Brothers Karamazov*. And the generally accepted notion that this marks the real beginning of the story of Russian fiction in England, has itself been one of the main obstacles in the way of a proper assessment. For in fact this influence was no more a sudden and disembodied manifestation than any other. There are important aspects and phases to be considered long before 1912, and there *is* a history, however fragmentary, lying behind it.

The concentration on the Dostoyevsky cult, which admittedly marks the climax of the fever itself, has led in fact to a further distortion of the true picture. The first step, therefore, in any examination of the reception of the Russian Novel in England, must be to shift the emphasis away from Dostoyevsky, and to place it instead on Turgenev.

There is, moreover, a pre-history which should not be entirely ignored. Although, for example, it is true that the majority of the earlier translations were unsatisfactory they did exist, and at a much earlier date than is usually realized. The first of them was a translation, apparently direct from the original, of the *Russian Catechism* of Prokopovich (1681–1736) made as early as 1723, while the starting-point of the history of Russian fiction in this country, from the purely chronological point of view, was the publication in 1793 of *Ivan Czarowitz : or the Rose Without Prickles that Stings Not*, one of the moral fables written by Catherine the Great (1729–1796).

Many of the earlier translations, it is true, are of greater interest to the bibliographer than to the literary historian, and only a few of them are relevant here. Sir John Bowring's *Specimens of the Russian Poets*, for example, published in 1821, and followed by a second part in 1823, can be considered as something of a landmark. It appears to have created a genuine burst of interest, and translations from the poets who had appeared in it, particularly Derzhavin (1743–1816), Zhukovsky (1783–1852) and Krylov (1769–1844) were fairly common in the periodicals throughout the nineteenth century, while in 1869 W. R. S. Ralston, undoubtedly the best of the early translators, published *Krilov and his Fables*. On the other hand the poetry of both Lermontov (1814–1841) and Pushkin (1799–1837) was poorly represented during this early period.

As far as fiction is concerned, some of the sentimental tales of Karamzin (1766–1826)—strongly influenced by Sterne—appeared in three separate translations in 1803. Several of Sir Walter Scott's Russian disciples were also translated: in 1831 for example Bulgarin's (1789–1859) *Ivan Vyzhigin* appeared in America, the first Russian novel to do so. Zagoskin's (1789–1852) *The Young Muscovite : or the Poles in Russia*, dedicated to Scott, appeared three years later, and rather more important because a wider public was involved, Thomas Budge Shaw's translation of *Ammalet Bek* by Marlinsky (i.e. A. Bestuzhev, 1797–1837) was published in *Blackwood's Edinburgh Magazine* in 1843.

The first spell of really sustained interest in Russian fiction, however, belongs to the period of the Crimean War, when the British public were for the first time introduced to Russian writers of great and original literary calibre.

The most important of this group of translations, from the point of view of the reputation of Russian fiction, was one of Pushkin's *Queen of Spades* (almost certainly taken from Prosper Merimée's translation in the *Revue des Deux Mondes* a few years earlier), and the form it took suggests a considerable audience at a more popular level, for it was published in October 1850 in *Chambers' Papers for the People*. It was reprinted the same year in the American periodical the *Living Age*, appeared again in 1854 in the *Gift of Friendship*, and maintained its popularity throughout the nineteenth century, with several new translations, and numerous reprints in magazines and periodicals, achieving its final apotheosis in the twentieth on the cinema screen. *The Captain's Daughter* (first translated in 1859) was almost as popular and in fact nearly all of Pushkin's prose tales had been translated by the end of the nineteenth century.

Lermontov's first appearance, on the other hand, illustrated only too clearly the distorting effect of political issues. For in 1853 a book entitled *Sketches of Russian Life in the Caucasus* was published, ascribed to a mysterious "Russe, Many Years Resident Among the Mountain Tribes" and purporting, for obvious propaganda purposes, to be a factual account. It was actually a pirated version, much mutilated, of Lermontov's *A Hero of Our Times*. It quickly recovered from this false start, for there were two complete versions the following year, and fresh versions followed at fairly regular intervals. But the fate of Gogol's great novel was not so fortunate. For the first translation of *Dead Souls* was another piracy, also considerably mutilated, and also propagandist in intention, published in 1854 under the title of *Home Life in Russia*. The author this time is described as "A Russian Noble" (in reality a Polish refugee living in Edinburgh), and the Preface proclaims that the intention of the book is to give "an insight into the internal circumstances and relations of Russian society which only a Russian could afford". It assures the reader that the story is absolutely true, and that "the main facts are well known in Russia". In other words the book is presented as a piece of straightforward reporting, and it was not until 1886 that *Dead Souls* was again translated by Isabel Hapgood and ascribed to Gogol (1809–1848) and even then it received scant justice, for a concocted *Continuation of Dead Souls*, vastly inferior in quality, was added without explanation, and this defect was not remedied until Constance Garnett published her version in 1922.

This brief and incomplete summary of the early translations is perhaps sufficient to show that quite a considerable body of Russian fiction was, even before 1869, available in translation. It is true that it made very little impact. The earlier prejudices, represented by John Milton's assertion in his *Brief History of Muscovia* (1682) that the Russians "have no learning, nor will suffer it to be among them" died hard, and most of the early translations were treated as little more than literary curios. The ignorance of the general public about Russian literature as a whole was abysmal throughout the nineteenth century and, if it comes to that, beyond it. Even the periodicals that discussed it committed many blunders. Nevertheless several of them did try to keep their readers informed, and regularly reviewed not only the English translations, but also the French and German, as well as the surveys of Russian literature that began to appear

B

in France and Germany at an early date. In 1824 the *Westminster Review* published a long article entitled "Politics and Literature in Russia" in its first number, and four years later the *Foreign Quarterly* published "Russian Literature and Poetry", which remained the standard account until in 1841 the *Westminster Review* edited by Sir John Bowring, published a new survey. These articles were reasonably accurate, and in 1845 *Blackwood's Edinburgh Magazine* began to publish articles and translations by Thomas Budge Shaw, a former lecturer in English at the Imperial Academy of Tsarkoe Selo, and a sound Russian scholar. Other periodicals too kept track of Russian literature while the *North American Review* began to publish notices in 1826.

These articles were not all of them patronizing. The Russian poets included in Bowring's anthology for example were on the whole very favourably received, and some of the early novels, Bulgarin's *Ivan Vejeyghen* (to use the curious transliteration of the 1831 translation) for example, were treated as respectable contributions to European fiction. Many of them were well aware that political prejudices were standing in the way of understanding, and a large number of them echoed the *Foreign Quarterly's* opinion of 1828 that although the existence of Russian literature "may be said to be of yesterday", for the future it was "full of hope and promise". The suddenness of the phenomenon was often stressed, and the note of awe that was to be so typical of those who imagined they had only just discovered Russian literature in 1912 is to be found quite early. Thus Sir John Bowring in his Advertisement to the second edition of his anthology speaks portentously of the "buds and blossoms of future expectation" to be found in contemporary Russian literature which "are scattered over half a world and in due time will ripen, to encourage, to console, and to stimulate myriads of millions".

Many of the early Russian novels of course were themselves derived from English models and on the whole it was these re-creations of the Scott or Byron formulae that proved most acceptable to English readers. This is indeed illustrated by the case of Gogol. For only one of his stories can be said to have received anything like a welcome. This was *Taras Bulba* (first translated in 1860 in a volume entitled *Cossack Tales*), a rousing adventure story set in the Ukraine, and obviously influenced by Scott.

Quite apart from the unfortunate circumstances attending the first appearance of *Dead Souls*, however, Gogol's work seems to have provoked hostility from the purely literary point of view.

"We should fall into very great error" (the *Westminster Review* wrote in 1841) "were we to estimate the state of intelligence among the educated classes in Russia from the popularity of such writers as Gogol . . . who dive to celebrity by writing down to the level of the lowest capacity . . . and whose seeming strength is no better than feebleness in hysterics",

and it dismisses the delightful *Old World Landowners* as "sans everything, except thorough inanity and feebleness".

The balance was somewhat redressed by the *Dublin University Magazine* which in September 1855 accompanied a translation of *Old World Landowners* (not the first of the tales to be translated, however, for *Blackwood's Edinburgh Magazine* had published a version of *The Portrait* in 1847) with a discussion of Gogol as a social critic, and as a victim of despotism. This is a most interesting example of the way in which a certain correspondence between social and economic conditions in Ireland and Russia produced a mutual sympathy for each other's literatures : Maria Edgeworth's stories of the peasants and landlords of County Longford, for example, had a considerable influence on Turgenev, whose *A Sportsman's Sketches* in turn possessed a particularly strong appeal for the Irish. But as far as England was concerned Gogol was a writer born out of his time. Of all the great Russian writers he was, as a matter of fact, the least touched himself by foreign influences ; and he was certainly "too Russian" for English readers of this period. His tales, as the *Westminster Review's* scathing comments suggest, were too strange in their narrative shape, and the "comedy" of *Dead Souls* was altogether too sombre for contemporary English tastes. It is significant too that Dostoyevsky, the Russian writer who admired him most, and who was closest to him spirit, did not appear in English translation until 1881 and in his turn received a somewhat grudging welcome.

In these early stages we are not of course looking for anything even remotely approaching a Russian influence—though even this, as we shall see later, took place very much earlier than is usually realized. But the first crude beginnings may be discerned nevertheless in the increasing number of romances with Russian themes and backgrounds. To take two representative examples as far back as 1806: *Demetrius: A Russian Romance* was derived from a French novel based in its turn upon Sumarakov's play, which was also translated into English in the same year, and *Elizabeth, or the Exiles of Siberia* was translated from a melodramatic romance by Mme Cottin full of the usual stereotyped background effects, and was later blamed by W. D. Howells as one of the books that "largely determined" early English and American attitudes.

There were also several cases of more direct borrowings, though nothing as thorough-going as that represented by a group. of novels by Alexandre Dumas *père* which were not far short of direct adaptations, without acknowledgment, of romances by Marlinsky. *The Governor's Daughter* by H. Sutherland Edwards (one of the earliest translators of Dostoyevsky) which was published in 1857, for example, has some obvious affinities with Zagoskin's *The Young Muscovite* and with Pushkin's *The Captain's Daughter*, and a book by a certain W. H. Patten-Saunders entitled *Black and Gold; or The Don! the Don!* published in 1864 dipped liberally for its effects into Gogol's *Taras Bulba*.

These examples are of no intrinsic importance: all they do is to show that the presence of a certain number of translations and a gradually growing awareness of Russian fiction had already begun to make themselves felt, and they can in consequence be regarded as the first stepping-stones towards the possible establishment of a Russian influence later on.

The most important event however in the early history of the Russian Novel in England, for reasons that will soon appear, was the arrival of Turgenev (1818–1883). The first translation of *A Sportsman's Sketches* it is true was a clumsy piracy, published in 1855 as *Russian Life in the Interior, or the Experiences of A Sportsman*, against which Turgenev vigorously protested. But in the previous year *Fraser's Magazine* had published *Photographs from Russian Life*, a perfectly respectable selection, with due acknowledgment of authorship, from Charrière's *Mémoires d'un Seigneur Russe*, and a year later *Household Words* under the editorship of Charles Dickens presented in its usual breezy manner a further selection, taken from the same source, under such titles as "The Children of the Tsar", "Nothing Like Russian Leather", and "A Singing Match", and in addition a complete version of *A Sportsman's Sketches*, also from the French, was published in the same year.

Turgenev's tales, moreover, from now on began to appear with increasing frequency in English and American periodicals, magazines, annuals and anthologies. And although in 1868 Turgenev had once more to protest against a piracy, of *Smoke : or Life at Baden-Baden*, two of his major novels appeared under the most favourable auspices. Thus in 1867 *Fathers and Sons* was published in New York, a translation from the Russian "with the approval of the author" by Eugene Schuyler, who had himself met Turgenev, and in 1869 W. R. S. Ralston, who was a personal friend of the author, published his *Liza* (with the sub-title : *A Nest of Nobles*, in the American edition of 1873) which can still rank as one of the most accurate and readable versions.

The tales of Pushkin and Lermontov, who were of course primarily poets, were welcomed mainly as interesting variations on Scottesque or Byronic themes : Gogol we have seen made an unfortunate start : Dostoyevsky (1828–1881) did not appear in translation until 1881 ; and although there was an authoritative translation from the Russian by the learned Malwida von Meysenburg of *Childhood and Youth* as early as 1862, Tolstoy (1828–1910) did not properly establish himself in translation until later in the century. But by 1869 a genuine demand for translations from Turgenev, though still within a very limited circle, was already making itself evident.

At this stage it is true the English Novel itself appeared to be in no need of "foreign stimulants", to use George Saintsbury's phrase. It was still to all outward appearances buoyantly confident in its own vitality and native resources, firmly rooted in an age of faith, stability and progress. It was only when the foundations of Victorian security showed signs of strain that writers began to question the assumptions on which the English Novel had been constructed, and to search for fictional forms and techniques more closely in touch with the problems of the day, and more "realistic" in their treatment of them, and when that time came they were no longer able to ignore the examples of other countries. That a choice was possible, however, was in large measure owing to the pioneer work of the handful of translators, scholars, critics and writers who first introduced Russian literature and Russian themes to the English public. And in the making of that choice it was above all the early establishment of Turgenev, symbolized by Ralston's *Liza*, that was to prove of primary importance.

CHAPTER TWO

AN OASIS WITH A MAGICAL FOUNTAIN

THE CHALLENGE OF REALISM—ENGLISH REACTIONS TO THE FRENCH NATURALISTS AND TO MELCHIOR DE VOGÜÉ'S BOOK ON THE RUSSIAN NOVEL

IN spite of the fact that the English Novel of the nineteenth century had so many great achievements to its credit, so that in retrospect it seems to present a picture of unusual confidence and coherence, it was really in a state of almost continuous adaptation and flux.

In the first place there were the rapid changes in the size and composition of the reading public, already evident in the first half of the century, and increasingly important as the Industrial Revolution gathered momentum and popular, and later compulsory, education was introduced.

> "A weary public," Rider Haggard declared, "calls continually for books, new books to make them forget, to refresh them, to occupy minds jaded with the toil and emptiness . . . and vexation of our competitive existence."

But what books? The question was an urgent one in a sense that had not existed in the eighteenth century when writers and readers were more or less united in tastes and standards. Now there were ever-widening breaches in the old unified tradition, so that by 1855 Cardinal Wiseman—in a way that would not have been possible in the preceding century—could split literature into separate compartments under the labels of "True, or High Literature", "Wholesome Popular Literature", "Trash and Garbage", "The Literature of Costermongers", and "Railway Literature".

To many of the more conservative critics, moreover, these boundaries were sufficiently wide to include many of the great

23

Victorian novelists themselves. It was not perhaps surprising that the Brontës at their first appearance should have seemed shocking—so that *Wuthering Heights* could be described in 1852 as "that wild, wilful and . . . wicked book", and *Jane Eyre* could be held out three years later as an "invasion" which had let loose the "most alarming revolution of modern times". It is more surprising, however, to find Trollope described as "uncompromisingly realistic", accused of "morbidity" and unpleasant "Pre-Raphaelitism", and even George Eliot's *Mill on the Floss* (1860) attacked by Ruskin in "Fiction Fair and Foul" (first published in the *Nineteenth Century* 1881–2) as "perhaps the most striking instance extant" of the modern "study of cutaneous disease".

While critics were agreed, therefore, that many of the tendencies of contemporary fiction were deplorable they were divided, both among themselves and in their own minds, as to what should and should not constitute the proper material for "serious" fiction.

This was a period in which criticism was dominated by "the young person" and the propriety of a piece of literature was to be measured by the degree to which it brought, or avoided bringing, a "mantling flush" to "the maiden cheek". Thus Thackeray complained in the Preface to *The History of Pendennis* (1848–50) that since the author of *Tom Jones* no English writer of fiction had been permitted "to depict to his utmost power a Man. We must drape him and give him a conventional simper. Society will not tolerate the Natural in our art."

But even those critics who subscribed most whole-heartedly to the conventions were disturbed by the lowering of vitality that seemed to accompany them. "It is a pity," *Fraser's Magazine* was complaining as early as 1851, "that morality should be rendered so excessively stupid on this side of the Channel," and that it should be accompanied by such a marked "absence of constitutional ardour". Even if an English novel did venture to touch on "doubtful" matters, the article continued, its "delinquencies" were comparatively safe, because they were "executed with a positive dreariness which repels imitation".

The issue of morality however was only one aspect of what the *Spectator* in 1887 so aptly described as "the great travail" of the nineteenth century—an age which was "restless in all its phases"—an age of "investigation without full confidence, either in its assumptions or its doubts". And the best of the nineteenth-century fiction reflected these doubts, and struggles, and all the impassioned seeking of the period.

The greatest challenge of all came from Science. "The whole of modern thought," Huxley said in his famous lecture "A Lobster; or the Story of Zoology", delivered at the South Kensington Museum on May 14, 1860, was steeped in science:

> "It has made its way into the works of our best poets, and even the mere man of letters who affects to ignore and despise science, is unconsciously impregnated with her spirit, and indebted for his best products to her methods. I believe that the greatest intellectual revolution mankind has yet seen is now slowly taking place by her agency. She is teaching the world that the ultimate court of appeal is observation and experiment and not authority; she is teaching it to estimate the value of evidence; she is creating a firm and living faith in the existence of immutable moral and physical laws, perfect obedience to which is the highest possible aim of an intelligent being."

The full force of the scientific challenge, as far as the Novel was concerned, was not fully realized until the advent of the French Naturalists. In France the idea of applying what might be called "scientific methods" to literature was nothing new. Diderot "The Father of French Realism" had come close to formulating it in his *Lettre sur les Aveugles* (1749) and in *La rêve d'Alembert* (published in 1830), and to practising it in some of his novels. "There is nothing good in this world but that which is true," had been his dictum, and it was also that of Balzac.

Balzac's reception in England in fact forms a kind of preview to that of the Naturalists. At first his version of the search for "the true", with its disregard of conventional morality, and of the limits traditionally regarded as proper to literature, inspired almost universal revulsion and the verdict of the *Quarterly Review* of April 1836—"a baser, meaner, filthier rascal never polluted society"—was typical.

Gradually, however, although in some quarters the hostility continued throughout the century, the attitude changed, and by 1875 we find Henry James writing of Balzac "Be the morality false or true, the writer's deference to it greets us as a kind of essential perfume", and Arthur Symons hailing him in 1899 as "One of those divine spies, for whom the world has no secrets", as an example of the kind of genius who "will find spirit everywhere".

The improvement in his reputation, moreover, was directly related to the far more drastic challenge represented by Zola and his fellow Naturalists : for if Balzac had subjected his material to a scrutiny akin to that of a scientist's in its thoroughness and boldness, they were "scientific" in a far more literal and alarming sense.

The manifesto of the movement was Zola's *Le Roman Experimental* published as a series of essays between 1875 and 1879, and deriving its direct inspiration from the work of Dr. Claude Bernard who had insisted that medicine, hitherto regarded as an art as much as a science, should submit itself to the same experimental disciplines as those of chemistry and physics. Zola applied Bernard's ideas to the art—or science—of fiction, arguing that the work of the novelist must follow much the same procedures as those of the scientist in his laboratory. He too must begin with observation of the facts—hence Zola's lavish use of the note-book method and his study of local conditions. These observed facts provided the solid ground on which the characters and events would move—and at this point the novelist instituted his "experiments", in other words he made his characters perform within a particular story, in order to demonstrate that their actions, and all the other events that ensued were "such as were required of the things studied". It followed that when once he had chosen his personages, scenes, environments and so on, the "scientific" novelist was in a certain sense a passive instrument—for as in chemistry or physics, when once the experiment had begun the rôle of the experimenter was confined to preserving the conditions necessary for success.

These ideas involved a realism of a more uncompromising kind than anything that had gone before, and clearly if their validity were to be accepted conventional "morality" could have no place in a realistic novel—it was simply a subjective irrelevance. For whereas the "idealist", according to Zola, claimed that it was necessary to lie in order to be moral, the Naturalists believed that it was impossible to be moral outside the boundaries of the scientifically true. "We teach the bitter science of life," Zola declared, "the uncompromising lesson of the real."

On the grounds of morality the Naturalistic doctrines were obviously bound to be repugnant to English readers and the publication of translations from Zola, Flaubert, the brothers Goncourt, Daudet, and Maupassant provoked a storm of public indignation. It was only too clear that the novels like *Nana* (1880) and *L'Assomoir* (1877) were *not* suitable for "the young person". "How can we expect the young to escape spring blights," the *Fortnightly Review* demanded, "if that beautiful guard against them, the sense which calls the mantling flush to the cheek, is broken down by literature that is wantonly purulent?" And to the *Quarterly Review* Zola's work appeared as a veritable "Chamber of Horrors", which had "a door leading into the shambles, the surgeon's hall of 'demonstration', the house of shame, the prison, the pawn-shop, the reeking tavern", a world "stricken with leprosy", suffused with a "nameless horror", and "fit only to be shovelled out of sight".

There were a few isolated champions of the French Naturalists. George Moore, for example, that chameleon of novelists, professed himself a follower, and Henry James gave his modified approval (though as we shall see both Moore and James later recanted). But for the most part the first reaction of English writers and critics was extremely hostile. Thus George Saintsbury, who had done so much to acquaint his countrymen with French realistic fiction, attacked Zola's "grossière étiquette", dismissed his theory of Naturalistic documentation as "wearisome nonsense" and dubbed him "the dirt-compeller". Even Swinburne, who had defended Baudelaire in a review of *Les Fleurs du Mal* in 1862 (the *Spectator*, September 6th) and whose own *Poems and Ballads* had been accused of vulgarity, paganism, brutality, bestiality, and general "unhealthiness", attacked *L'Assomoir*.

The issue however was not merely one of prudery, and the story of Zola's reception in England throws into relief all the doubts and searchings of a period struggling to reconcile the claims of Science with those older faiths and traditions, which were still a matter of instinct rather than of ratiocination. Of all the challenges which the Victorians had been called upon to face, that of Naturalism was perhaps the most severe. Serious writers had been prepared to accept the exhortation implied in Huxley's lecture of 1860—to be "realistic" in their approach to the spirit of the times. Naturalism was a different matter: even the boldest shrank from the implications of *Le Roman Experimental*.

What these implications were it was only too easy to see. W. S. Lilley, for example, in a vigorous onslaught on "The New Naturalism" (the *Fortnightly Review*, 1885) listed them as

> "the banishing from human life of all that gives it glory and honour: the victory of fact over principle, of mechanism over imagination: of appetite dignified as rights over duties: of sensation over intellect; of the belly over the heart, of fatalism over moral freedom: of brute force over justice; in a word of *matter over mind*".

Naturalistic fiction, in fact, was the literary counterpart of all the scientific and philosophical ideas which most seriously threatened the foundations of Victorian stability and peace of mind.

Among the general public the feeling against Zola and his followers was even more violent than among the writers and critics. It found a mouthpiece in the National Vigilance Association, which launched a campaign against "immoral" literature, concentrating its attacks on Henry Vizetelly, the principal English publisher of the French Naturalists—though in its zeal it also condemned a wide range of books, including the "Mermaid" editions of the minor Elizabethan dramatists.

The campaign reached its climax when on May 10th, 1888, Samuel Smith, at the instigation of the National Vigilance Association, proposed in the House of Commons, that "this House deplores the rapid spread of demoralizing literature, and is of the opinion that the law against indecent publications and pictures should be enforced, and if necessary strengthened". The motion was carried unanimously, and was followed by an outcry in the popular press, which accused Zola and his fellow

Naturalists of "dangerous lubricity", of setting out "to sap the foundations of manhood and womanhood", of having "not only destroyed innocence, but corroded the moral nature", and of having "simply wallowed in immorality", to quote a few representative comments from the London and provincial daily press. The National Vigilance Association secured an indictment of Vizetelly for "trafficking in pornographic literature". He was convicted, fined and put on probation for a year. In 1889 the Association again brought him to court, for continuing to publish translations (though much bowdlerized) of the French Naturalists, and this time he was sentenced to three months' imprisonment.

And yet how typical it was of the period, with its divided conscience, its philosophical dilemmas, its determination to search for the truth and its fear of being afraid of the consequences —and, over and above the torturing doubts, its courage and vitality—that a petition protesting against Vizetelly's imprisonment was signed by 125 leading men of letters, including many who, like Hall Caine, had been particularly virulent in their attacks on the French novelists.

The attacks, it is true, continued in many quarters, but popular interest in the controversy gradually waned during the 1890s, and translations of Zola and the other French Naturalists returned to the publishers' lists. Many of the critics adopted a more tolerant attitude. Edmund Gosse, for example, boldly proclaimed Zola as "the one living novelist who has movement of life". And we almost rub our eyes in astonishment when we read in the *Fortnightly Review*, under the heading "Zola's Philosophy of Life", that yesterday's monster of depravity now apparently "holds out the promise of a better world", and that Vernon Lee has written an article entitled "The Moral Teaching of Zola"! Even more astonishing, perhaps, is the fact that in 1893 Zola himself was fêted in London as the guest of the Institute of Journalists.

By 1896 the active controversy was over. It was no longer necessary to plead the cause of the Naturalists, and they could count on a considerable audience of English readers. What was more, a whole series of novels—among them Henry Harland's *Mlle Miss*, Hubert Crackenthorpe's *Wreckage*, George Egerton's

Keynotes, Richard Whiteing's *No. 5 John Street*, Arthur Morrison's *Children of the Jago*, George Moore's *Esther Waters*, and Mr. Somerset Maugham's *Liza of Lambeth*—was closely influenced by Naturalist precepts and practices.[1] It looked as if the whirligig of taste had performed one of its most spectacular revolutions, as if English Realism, after all its doubts and self-searchings, had turned towards the French solution.

But how deep was this change of heart? Certainly there could be no doubt that Zola's work had administered an invigorating shock to English fiction, helping to jerk it out of its insularity, destroying the belief that literature was somehow sacrosanct, divorced from sordid realities, focusing contemporary fiction upon the social problems of the day, and revealing a wider range of experience. The English Novel could never be quite the same again : as Edmund Gosse put it, English writers had "eaten of the apple of knowledge", and would not in future be content with "mere marionettes".

Nevertheless it was soon evident that a reaction against Zola and the Naturalists was under way. It had been signalled by two articles in the *Yellow Book*—Arthur Waugh's "Reticence in Literature" in 1893, and Arthur Symons' "A Note on Zola's Method" in the following year. Zola, Symons declared, in spite of his truthfulness and honesty, "sickened" the reader with "plebeian flesh"; there was about his work "something greasy, a smell of eating and drinking"; he saw the world through a "formula", and worst crime of all—his fingers were "too thick", they left "a blurred line".

The Aesthetic Movement in fact, although it was in full agreement with the Naturalists' attack on conventional morality, and although Flaubert became one of its idols by virtue of his preoccupation with "style", set itself against the doctrine of "usefulness" and "truthfulness" in Art.

Other influences worked in a similar direction. "Romantic" voices were raised for the first time for several years : . . . "if the battle between the crocodile of Realism and the catawampus of Romance is to be fought out to the bitter end, why . . . I am on the side of the catawampus", Andrew Lang proclaimed. There was a revival of the novel of adventure, and Robert Louis

[1] Some critics have suggested that Russian influences can also be detected.

Stevenson argued that the great danger of Realism was its proneness to sacrifice "the beauty and significance of the whole to
local dexterity". The Celtic Movement and the influence of the
French Symbolists also contributed to the reaction. Above all, the
earlier faith in the infallibility of Science had been weakened ;
developments in biology which stressed individual variation
rather than natural selection had helped to break up the deter-
minism which had been important from the point of view of
Naturalistic characterization, and there was a revival of "idealism" in philosophy, criticism, and literature.

There can be no mistaking the accents of relief with which
the majority of critics and writers explored the new arguments.
They are apparent, alike, in Hall Caine's "fiction . . . is fallacy,
poetic fallacy, a lie if you like, a beautiful lie, a lie that is at once
false and true—false to fact, true to faith" ; in Julia Wedgwood's
"When literature exchanges the selective touch of morals, for
the collective grasp of science, she abandons her true vocation"
and in Vernon Lee's belief in "a kind of conscience of beautiful
and ugly" analogous to "that other conscience of right and wrong".

These were voices that expressed instinctive English reactions
and preferences. The swing in the direction of Naturalism was,
in fact, a passing phase : it was fundamentally alien to English
tastes and temperaments.

This was far from implying, however, that the concept of
Realism in fiction had been defeated in spite of local gains by
the Romantics. It merely pointed to the fact that the English
Novel had looked at Naturalism and found it wanting. But
Hubert Crackenthorpe was right in saying that serious novelists
had no intention of returning to the "pleasant fallacies" of the
"well made plot", and the search for forms of Realism more
consonant to English tastes and traditions continued. The
challenge in fact remained.

.   .   .   .   .

It was from France itself that the answer came. There the
battle over Naturalism raged as fiercely as in England—and
influential voices, in particular that of Brunetière, had all along
been raised against Zola and his followers.

At first, it is true, the triumph of the Naturalists seemed assured. Zola himself enjoyed great personal popularity and his novels had huge sales. But gradually a reaction set in, and in August 1887 *Figaro* published a "Manifesto of the Time" in which a number of minor Naturalists announced their defection from the movement. There were disagreements too among the "solid core" of the Naturalists; Huysmans, for example, angered Zola by his conversion to Catholicism and the publication of his religious novel *A Rebours*, and Daudet, whose membership of the group had always been equivocal (and who alone among the Naturalists met with a warm welcome on his first appearance in England), proclaimed that he had lost interest in the Naturalist approach and wished to devote himself to a fiction of "happiness". And when in 1891 Jules Huret conducted an "inquest" on Naturalism for the *Écho de Paris*, in which he asked a representative group of novelists for their views on the present state and future prospects of Naturalism, the answers clearly showed that the reaction was well under way, and that new influences were in the ascendant. Bergson's *Essai sur les Données Immédiates de la Conscience* (1889), for example, with its exposition of the qualitative nature and "fluidity" of reality, exercised an increasingly powerful appeal. Novels such as Pierre Loti's *Pêcheur d'Islande* (1886), and Paul Bourget's *Le Disciple* (1889), showed the "idealist" trend of events, and Rémy de Gourmont in the *Mercure de France* insisted that the new generation was opposed to Naturalism, that it departed "with disgust" from a literature "whose baseness makes us vomit" and proclaimed—"Villiers de l'Isle-Adam is our Flaubert! Laforgue and Mallarmé are our masters!"

But in France, as in England, the search for an "acceptable" form of Realism still continued, and it is in this context that the work of Eugène Melchior, Vicomte de Vogüé (1848–1910) must be considered. His studies of Russian literature began in the *Revue des Deux Mondes* in March 1879, but it was the series of articles on the Russian Novel, commencing in October 1883, and published in book form as *Le Roman Russe* in 1886, which formed his major work.

The Avant-Propos, together with the introductory chapters, constituted one of the outstanding manifestos of the anti-Natural-

istic Movement. Realism, de Vogüé pointed out in them, performed an important function in modern life because it met the
desire of the public for forms more in accordance with the
positive science of the day—forms that would tell them more
about the complexities of emotional life, the minutiae of day-
to-day existence, the interrelations of human beings to each
other and to society as a whole. But, he insisted, Realism could
command respect only if it fulfilled one vital condition—that it
submit itself to religious and spiritual values. For Realism
"insulted, and deceived" our "innate instincts" if it ignored
the existence of a Divine Power governing and directing a universe which, in spite of Science's arrogant claims, was fundamentally beyond our understanding. Realism must recognize that
man's naïve belief that all knowledge was within his grasp had
been discounted : that his ignorance grew in proportion : that the
faith in Science which Zola professed was an illusion : that man
had in fact been able to roll back "la ceinture des ténèbres" but an
infinitesimal distance : and that faced with the pitiful limitations
of his powers, he must again fill the empty spaces which he
himself had created with the God whom he himself had expelled.

It was the recognition of these facts alone, de Vogüé insisted,
that could justify the "harshness" of the methods of Realism.
If it set out to examine at close quarters the horrors and miseries
of the world, it must relieve them by compassion and by charity,
otherwise it would become arrogant, nihilistic, and "utterly
odious". Of all the manifestations of art, in fact, Realism was
the most in need of the religious sentiment.

Unfortunately for her literature, the whole intellectual
tradition of France, de Vogüé argued, was opposed to that
aesthetic which alone could secure the health and survival
of Realism. The majority of French Realists, in fact, had ignored
"the best half of the world".

Was it possible, then, to point to examples of modern Realism
which *did* possess the saving graces which the French lacked,
and which fulfilled the conditions which he had laid down as
absolutely essential? They could be found in two countries—in
England and in Russia.

In both these countries, de Vogüé believed, "the soul was
in the right condition" to receive Realism, and "everything

C

favoured its growth". For example—whereas the Latin genius was for "the absolute", the Anglo-Saxon and Slav genius was for "the relative" : whereas the French isolated a fact or character, the Anglo-Saxon and the Slav "felt the necessity to deal with the whole complex world" in its spiritual no less than its material manifestations.

In England at the very moment when Flaubert's "waning intellect" was introducing modern Realism into France, novelists such as George Eliot were exemplifying its true use, and carrying the tradition initiated by Richardson on to its "most glorious" phase.

The English Novel owed its "high moral tone" to its "religious foundations". This was true, moreover, even in its "most cynical" productions—for the most daring Realism was permissible, only provided it was suffused by spiritual light. George Eliot could put forward highly unconventional views, and even discard the old faith—but in spite of it she had in her blood what Montégut had called "cette monade religieuse première", that primary religious drop, which was deposited in every English mind by Protestantism. Whereas the French Realists only went skin-deep, there was "no corner of the human heart" to which the English had not penetrated, for their work, as Brunetière had said, was permeated by "sympathie de l'intelligence éclairée par l'amour" —and this quality of mind and soul alone provided the proper instrument for psychological analysis.

Turning to the Russian Novel, de Vogüé declared that the closest possible correspondence existed between Russian and English Realism. They even shared the same defects, of diffuseness in structure and lack of "composition". In spite of these minor weaknesses they were both infinitely superior to French Realism. It was indeed significant that the Russians owed so much to Dickens and so little to Balzac.

As far as the treatment of "wretchedness and despair" was concerned, the Russians could in fact claim the doubtful honour of priority. But they had soon outgrown any excesses in this respect, while the French Realists, and Flaubert in particular, "laboriously plodded" further and further along the road to pessimism and nihilism.

The Russian Realists in fact, like the English, were moved

always by a moral principle, and by a compassion "filtrée de tout élément impur, et sublimée par l'esprit évangélique", and it was for these reasons, de Vogüé declared, that Russian fiction had gradually penetrated European consciousness—for here was a type of Realism which was fully in accord with "the spirit of the age" and responded to all the demands of "real life" at the same time that it answered to the fundamental needs of the human soul. The Russians in fact had "pleaded the cause of Realism with new arguments"—arguments which provided the only possible answer to the challenge of Naturalism.

De Vogüé's book was an important event in the French literary and aesthetic controversy. But it is obvious too that his arguments had a special relevance for the English. *Le Roman Russe* itself did not in fact appear in translation in England until 1913, though there was an early American edition. But de Vogüé's work was well known in England. The studies in the *Revue des Deux Mondes* (notably those on Dostoyevsky in 1885) were, for example, the obvious inspiration behind several articles in the English periodicals.

While the controversy over Naturalism had been raging, moreover, the efforts of the early pioneers had been bearing fruit, and the translations of Russian novels had steadily accumulated. From 1869 until the end of the century scarcely a year passed without several fresh ones appearing. In 1886, counting separate editions, no less than eighteen Russian titles appeared in London and New York; and in the following year the total was at least twenty. By the end of this decade all the great Russian novelists were represented in English versions, and most of their major works had been translated.

At one point admittedly it looked as if the Russian Realists might be tarred with the same brush as the French. Some of them, for example, appeared on Henry Vizetelly's lists at a time when the zeal of the National Vigilance Association was still at its height. There were complaints, both in England and America, that the Russians were too "melancholy", "sombre", or "pessimistic". "The effect of Russian fiction", the *Saturday Review* observed in 1887, was "mostly wretchedness", and the *Quarterly Review* in 1891 attacked those who rated Tolstoy and Dostoyevsky above Balzac and Thackeray, and lumped together

Tolstoy's *The Kreutzer Sonata* (1889), Zola's *La Terre* (1887) and the plays of Ibsen as equally objectionable. George Saintsbury also asserted that the Russians were "grimy", and that there was "too much healthiness and beefiness in the English temperament" for it ever to indulge in "the sterile pessimism which seems to dominate Russian fiction".

On the whole however, from 1869 onwards, the Russians received a warm welcome from writers and critics alike (although Saintsbury was unrepentant and kept up a running fight well into the twentieth century). What was more, a careful distinction was from the outset made between French and Russian Realism—even before de Vogüé came on the scene. When, for example, in 1869, the *North British Review* wrote about Ralston's *Liza*, it stressed Turgenev's "purity of tone", and told its readers that "it must never be supposed" that the Russian writer was "ever in the habit of copying the novelists of the French school". His tales in fact offered "a refreshing contrast" to their "cynical sensuality".

The contrast between the two types of Realism was developed in greater detail and profundity as de Vogüé's work became known. English critics seized, in particular, upon his analysis of the part played by *pity* and *hope* in the novels of the Russians, as opposed to the "barren pessimism" of the French. The Russians knew how to put vice under the microscope as well as the French, but they were exempt from "the strange colour-blindness of the soul which makes virtue invisible". For example, they too could feel the fascination and sombre power of Death, and they could express it with "unsurpassed power"—but at the same time "the mystery of suffering life and its strife with evil" had an even greater attraction for them: the wind from the graveyard might blow through their writings, but "a fresher wind from the lands of hope" pushed it aside (*London Quarterly Review*, April 1888).

This was indeed a far cry from the earlier patronage. Echoes of it were still apparent in the 1860s and 1870s and throughout the century we find side by side with enthusiastic comments complaints of ignorance and neglect. The whole process of infiltration in fact was extremely patchy. But at least Russian novels could no longer be regarded as literary curios, collectors' pieces emanating from a distant and half-civilized country, and their range, scope, and depth were increasingly stressed. Thus *Temple Bar* in 1890 declared that the Russian Novel contained within its borders examples of poetry, history, and psychology such as the world had "never equalled for minuteness of accuracy, and power"—and that it must be recognized as "a marvellous instrument of culture and progress". At the same time the special relevance to English literature was pointed out. Hall Caine, for example, declared that Tolstoy had taken all that was good in the Realism of France and "grafted it on to the brave and noble surpassing idealism of English poetry at the beginning of the century". The *London Quarterly* proclaimed that the Russian novelists were as much part of the age as Byron, Dickens, Thackeray and George Eliot, and the *Spectator*, pointing to their "religious intensity", believed that the Englishman, if he desired "perfection", would "have to learn of the Russian".

In this sudden enhancing of the status of the Russian Novel the authority of Matthew Arnold played a considerable part. It was he, according to the *Westminster Review*, who had aroused Englishmen from their "satisfaction with things British and provincial", and one of the results of his efforts was that Tolstoy's name was no longer familiar only to a select circle, no longer merely "caviare to the circulating library", but had also reached "the ears of the profane crowd".

His article on Tolstoy, which appeared in the December 1887 issue of the *Fortnightly Review* (and was reprinted in the second series of *Essays in Criticism*), like de Vogüé's Avant-Propos to *Le Roman Russe* (which of course Arnold had read) set out to expose the limitations of "a severe and pitiless truth as the last word of experience". In spite of the careful observation, maturity and force of the French Realists, there was, Arnold felt, "a touch of hardness" in their work, and in consequence the French Novel had lost much of the appeal which it formerly possessed for educated Europeans.

Thus Flaubert's *Madame Bovary* seemed to him fundamentally a work of "petrified feeling". Against it he set Tolstoy's *Anna Karenina*. In many respects the two novels were similar, and as far as the "realism" of treatment was concerned Arnold regretted that Tolstoy had not been more "reticent". But though *Anna Karenina* exhibited a world which misconducted itself almost as much as that of a French novel—"all palpitating with 'modernity'", the Russian novel could be "advantageously distinguished" from the French. For although Tolstoy dealt with "criminal passion", he did not "feel himself owing any service to the goddess Lubricity, or bound to put in touches at this goddess's dictation". The "taint" which was so much in evidence in *Madame Bovary* was in fact "wholly absent" in *Anna Karenina*. Whereas "an atmosphere of bitterness, irony, impotence" hung over Flaubert's novel, and the "springs of freshness" were absent, in Tolstoy's was to be found the "treasures" of compassion, tenderness, and insight.

To Arnold Flaubert exemplifies the drying up of the idealistic and lyrical vein and he does not have de Vogüé's confidence in the powers of English fiction to counteract it. On the contrary, he believes that "the famous English novelists have passed away and left no successors of like fame". And in consequence he believes "it is not the English Novel that has inherited the vogue lost by the French" but that "of a country new to literature, or at any rate unregarded till lately by the general public of readers". It is in fact "the novel of Russia, which now has the vogue, and deserves to have it", and "if fresh literary productions maintain this vogue and enhance it, we shall all be learning Russian".

The recurrence of this theme of exhaustion in retrospect seems as surprising for the 1880s, when according to Sir Compton Mackenzie the English Novel "sunk to its nadir", as when we encountered it in connection with the early decades of the century. Nevertheless when we find these complaints of exhaustion in conjunction with articles on Russian fiction, it is reasonable to suppose that the conditions for literary influence are present. Certainly Arnold's essay was by no means an isolated instance. The *Westminster Review* of September 1888 (in an article entitled "Count Tolstoi's Life and Works") posed the question "Why should the countrymen of Richardson, Scott and Dickens" be forced to look far afield "for example in fiction?" and offered as answer—"the decline of our native novel". And it comes to much the same conclusion as Arnold—"for the moment, Russia takes the position which England held in the seventeenth and France in the eighteenth century".

There were other writers too to drive home the lessons of de Vogüé's book. C. E. Turner, for example, who wrote an important series of articles on the Russian novelists for *Fraser's Magazine* in 1877, and whose *Studies in Russian Literature* was published in 1882, followed by *Modern Novelists in Russia* in 1890, was representative of a new element in the attitude towards Russian literature: the period of serious and scholarly study had begun. Among the reviewers of the 1890s, for example, was William Morfill, the pioneer of Slavonic Studies at Oxford University, and other specialists in Slavonic languages were soon to begin their work, including Bernard Pares who inaugurated the School of Russian Studies at Liverpool University in 1907 (and who was later associated with the School of Slavonic Studies at King's College, London). And it was in the 1890s, of course, that Edward and Constance Garnett began to set an entirely new standard of translation. Lecture courses on Russian literature too were becoming increasingly popular, particularly in America. Nathan Haskell Dole, for example, and Isabel Hapgood, the translator of Turgenev, conducted lectures and study groups for the Chautauqua Circles in 1902. Other courses were by Russian exiles living in America, among them Ivan Panin, Serge Wolkonsky, and P. A. Kropotkin (1842–1921)—whose lectures appeared in book form in England and America. At the same time such important European studies as Ernest Dupuy's *Les Grands Maîtres de la Littérature Russe* (almost as influential as de Vogüé's book, according to some critics) and Georg Brandes' *Impressions of Russia* were translated into English.

During the 1880s and 1890s, in other words, Russian literature firmly established itself. In America the process was perhaps steadier than in England, largely because of the absence, at that date, of distracting political rivalries. In American literary circles indeed there was something approaching a "Russian craze", and the number of translations during this period rose even more steeply than in England: by 1889 there were, for example, twenty-seven editions of Tolstoy's novels and tales, representing sixteen different titles, and twenty-one separate translations; and according to the *Westminster Review* for September 1888 "rival translations" of his books were "competing for sale in Boston as they compete in Paris".

The search for "true realism", reflecting as it did so much of the passionate seeking of the period, however, was by no means over. As late as 1919 Arnold Bennett was still arguing that the orientation of the English Novel towards its own brand of Realism was not complete (in one sense of course it is a process that can never be complete, so long as there are writers passionately concerned to explore the truths of human experience). But after the brief spell of "whistling in the dark", in which English novelists had experimented with the methods of Naturalism, it was clear that the French model would not serve. With their inherent honesty and determination to face the challenges of their time the Victorians had reluctantly approached what Edmund Gosse described as "the Scylla and Charybdis of Naturalism". But there can be no mistaking the frame of mind with which they greeted the alternative offered by the Russians. There is the joy of discovery in a pronouncement in the *Athenaeum* in 1887 that the English people have just found a "new vein of gold, this strange and fairylike thing called Russian literature, and the mine is being eagerly worked". The same tone of relief in the realization that a way of escape is open is apparent in the declaration in *Temple Bar* that "to-day the Russians are our masters in a new school—we can sit at their feet and learn". It would be incorrect to ascribe the credit for this discovery entirely to de Vogüé: as we have seen the English were quick to draw the distinction between French and Russian Realism for themselves. But there can also be little doubt that *Le Roman Russe* had performed a signal service for the whole of Europe, and for England perhaps in particular.

Looking back over the controversy in 1910 Edmund Gosse provided perhaps the most convincing evidence of its impact, when he described it as "one of the most powerfully influential products of literary criticism in the nineteenth century", as "the most epoch-making single volume of criticism issued in France during our time", and as "a revelation of the most blazing order". For it was de Vogüé, Gosse pointed out, who had discovered for Europe a school of Realists, no less serious and thorough in its methods than Zola and his followers, but admitting far more "spiritual unction" into their approach to life. He had shown us undoubted "masters" of modern fiction fully aware of the demands of truth, but refusing to move a single step towards it "without being attended by pity and hope". He had, declared Gosse, raised a rallying cry for all those souls "who had wandered in the night of Naturalism". From the "dry positivism" of the Naturalistic Law there had seemed no appeal until de Vogüé came to the rescue. He had come at a time when "weariness and emptiness had fallen upon the fields of literature" and had "called down once more upon them the dews of virtue and beauty". He would be remembered, Gosse declared, because "when weariness had fallen upon the world of letters, he discovered an oasis with a magical fountain in it".

CHAPTER THREE

A NEST OF GENTLEFOLK AT SIX MILE BOTTOM

THE lamps have just been lit in a typical country house in the village of Six Mile Bottom not far from Newmarket. So recently that the light has not yet filled every corner of the room, and the guests are still conscious of the reflections of flames leaping on the walls and on the window-panes, and of the cold twilight outside. It is late in October, the most beautiful month of all in Cambridgeshire, even though the air is a little sharper and smokier, the Autumn atmosphere a little sadder than elsewhere in England. And in the sky—which is higher and wider than anywhere else in England—the fawns and silvers of noonday have changed to saffron and umber, and the darkness that gathers at its edges has a brown powdery texture, like soot. In the brief interval before night falls, black and deep like the waves of the North Sea, which indeed stand higher in many places than the fen country itself, a bat wheels: a curlew calls: the dogs stir and whine.

It is the time of the day, and the time of the year, when a sportsman is filled with a contentment, rendered more piquant by a tinge of melancholy, as he crosses the flat, spiky fields, or trudges along lanes on which the sweat drawn out by the pale midday sunshine is just turning into an icy film, with his gun under his arm, and his dog at his heel—or, better still, savours these last moments as, like the guests of Mr. Bullock Hall, he sits in the drawing-room, looking through the darkening squares of the window, waiting for dinner to be announced.

It is a typically English scene. But the atmosphere, the pastel colourings, the air of tender melancholy, seem to belong also to Turgenev, the landlord of Spasskoye, and the author of *A Sports-*

man's Sketches (1852),[1] while the country house with its distinguished gathering, which includes a Member of Parliament, an editor of Lucretius (an accidental overtone one presumes)—and George Henry Lewes and George Eliot—might almost have been the manor-house of Spasskoye—or any other "Nest of Gentlefolk". And the guest of honour whom they have come to meet is indeed Ivan Sergeyevich Turgenev. . . .

But now George Henry Lewes proposes the toast to "Europe's greatest living novelist". The "Russian giant" however rises to his feet, an imposing figure with his huge shoulders, the great lion-shaped head with its flowing white hair and beard and the broad flat nose, and speaking in his "slow broken English" repudiates the compliment, and insists on transferring it to "Europe's greatest living novelist"—George Eliot.

It is true that the authority for this particular incident is Oscar Browning who is not the most reliable of authorities. But it is a pleasing one to contemplate. It is pleasant too to imagine the party in the drawing-room after dinner, cut off from the flat East Anglian countryside, dark now and inhospitable with its biting October night wind, discussing life and literature and (according to Oscar Browning) listening to Turgenev as, in Russian this time, he reads verses from Pushkin. . . . And, whatever the authenticity of the account, the scene is one which symbolizes the hold which Turgenev has always had on English affections, and the very special place he occupies in the history of the Russian Novel in England.

The simple fact of his physical presence counts for a good deal. This particular gathering which according to Oscar Browning was in October 1878, though George Eliot's letters suggest that it took place two years earlier, was not his first, and neither was it the first meeting with George Eliot and G. H. Lewes. Turgenev was already, on the testimony of George Eliot's husband, J. W. Cross, a "very highly valued" friend; indeed Lewes, according to an entry in his Diary for January 8, 1871, first met Turgenev as long ago as 1839 (presumably in Germany). Turgenev's first visit to England, however, was in 1847, in company with the Viardots. Other visits followed and in 1860 he was staying at Ventnor in the Isle of Wight, where according to a letter of

[1] They began to appear in one of the Russian periodicals in 1847.

18th August he conceived the character of Bazarov and began the preliminary planning of *Fathers and Children* (1862).[1]

The primary object of some of these visits was to meet Alexander Herzen (i.e. Gertsen, 1812–1870), who had settled in London in 1852 in order to devote himself to his revolutionary paper *The Bell*. But he never held himself aloof from the English as Herzen had done. It was while he was at Holles Street, for example, that Thackeray was "greatly flattered and much moved" by a visit from Turgenev. In the same year he attended the annual dinner of the Royal Literary Fund at St. Martin's Hall, in company with Prosper Merimée, and during these earlier visits he met many Englishmen of letters and of affairs including Disraeli, Macaulay, and Carlyle; the latter took a particular liking to him and described him after he had been his guest at Melchet Court in 1870 as "a general favourite with high and low".

The year 1870–1871 is indeed an important one as regards these personal contacts between Turgenev and the English. He arrived in the Autumn of 1870, in company with the Viardots. It was "a lugubrious winter",[2] he wrote, but there were many social gatherings, particularly in the homes of D. G. Rossetti, and Ford Madox Ford—and of course there was always the shooting in Cambridgeshire. In July, too, he dined at Trinity College, Cambridge, and afterwards attended a debate at the Union—the subject, discussed with a phlegm that astonished him, was "Do the French Communards deserve the sympathy of Englishmen?"

At the Scott Centenary Celebrations that Summer, he himself spoke as the Russian representative—and for his pains was reported as "Torqueneff" in the *Scotsman* on the following day (August 10th). From Edinburgh he went on to the Highlands for the grouse shooting, meeting Robert Browning, Jowett, and Swinburne.

The climax to his personal contact with the English scene was reached in 1879, the year in which Turgenev arrived at the zenith of his fame, at home as well as abroad. His presence at

---

[1] To use now the more familiar title of Constance Garnett's translation.

[2] Most of the quotations from Turgenev's letters, articles, prefaces, etc., are taken from *Turgenev, the Man and His Art* (Yarmolinsky) or from *Turgenev: A Life* (Magarshack).

the Pushkin celebrations in Moscow had turned into a personal triumph and many European men of letters in sending telegrams to mark the occasion addressed them as a signal mark of respect to Turgenev himself. But on June 14th he was back in England in order to receive from the University of Oxford the honorary degree of Doctor of Civil Law. In introducing him, the Regius Professor spoke of his "wonderful genius, which was shown in his romances, and his descriptions of Russian life, which had led to the emancipation of the serfs", and although Turgenev feared that English hatred of Russia might cause "a rowdy scene", he was pleasurably surprised to find himself, as *The Times* confirmed the following day, "applauded more than the others".

On several of the later visits his friend and translator, W. R. S. Ralston, with whom he kept up a regular correspondence and who had visited him both at Baden-Baden and (in the summer of 1870) at Spasskoye, organized dinner-parties in his honour. At these, and at similar gatherings, he met many contemporary English novelists including Trollope, R. D. Blackmore, James Payn, and Walter Besant. Surprisingly enough, however, there is no evidence of a meeting with Dickens, although Dickens, as we have seen, was one of the first English editors to publish translations from *A Sportsman's Sketches*, while Turgenev, like all the Russian novelists, held Dickens in especial reverence. We know too that in 1863 Turgenev attended three of his public readings (and was "reduced to the ecstasies of a calf"), and that Dickens was an ardent admirer of Pauline Viardot, attending her concerts in London and in Paris and dining with her on several occasions.

The last of the dinner-parties in Turgenev's honour was in 1881—and it is a fitting curtain to this brief account of his contacts with England and the English that this, his last visit, was also primarily in the rôle of a sportsman—to shoot partridges, in Autumn, in Cambridgeshire.

In many ways, of course, Turgenev must have seemed a strange and alien figure. And there were times when he found the English every bit as puzzling as Herzen had done, describing them in a letter to the poet Fet (1821-1892) as "Wonderful, odd, majestic, stupid—all at once, and above all totally foreign to us". He noted too that politically the English "hate us terribly", and indeed in this year—it was just after the Treaty of Berlin—Russophobia was again at its most virulent, and Turgenev himself (perhaps at Six Mile Bottom after a day with his dog and his gun) wrote his only known jingoistic poem, *Croquet at Windsor*. It must be remembered too that his work at this stage was still known only to a small (though influential) circle: indeed Edmund Gosse later related that at some of the literary gatherings conversation was embarrassingly handicapped, because many of the English novelists assembled to meet their distinguished Russian contemporary had not read a single line he had written.

In this respect Turgenev was very much at an advantage. "I know English literature well, and I speak English fluently," he wrote to Ralston (October 1866). "He had a sound knowledge of English literature," George Moore reported of his conversation with Turgenev in Paris in 1879; "Shakespeare he had by heart, Burns he wanted to introduce to his compatriots, and Dickens delighted him immeasurably." Nevertheless, in spite of limitations and reservations on both sides, there was a real warmth in his dealings with the English and the very fact that he had talked face to face with many of them certainly played a part in creating a favourable climate of opinion for his works and ultimately for the Russian Novel in general.

It would perhaps be fanciful to suggest Sport as one of the operative factors. But the fact that the first of Turgenev's books to become known was entitled *A Sportsman's Sketches*, and that so many of his visits took in sporting excursions, is not without relevance. For it brought him closer: it displayed him in a rôle which appealed to English tastes—J. W. Cross, for example, in noting the 1876 visit to Six Mile Bottom, was quite sure that Turgenev had come to England in order "to compare his experiences of Russian and English sport"; it seemed a perfectly natural and adequate reason. That Turgenev possessed the tastes of an English country squire in fact did him no disservice. On the contrary, it contributed towards making him a really acceptable ambassador in the cause of Russian literature. His presence at Six Mile Bottom, "for the shooting", make it clear that he was himself a gentleman, of a type not so very different from the nineteenth-century English conception of the term. The point is well established by an article in *Blackwood's Edinburgh Magazine* in 1880 which, commenting on "the Turgenev cult", suggested that there were "certain similarities" between the English and Russian squirearchy, between "the tea urn and the samovar". English readers, the article pointed out, would have no difficulty in appreciating "the soft morning leisure" and "the cool dewy evenings", or the landscape of fields, woods, and remote villages clustered round "the little great house".

It is true that *A Sportsman's Sketches* was not just a book for sportsmen, but also a daring social document. It is true too that much of the early interest in Turgenev was concerned with politics. The long article in the *British Quarterly Review* of March 1869, for example (probably by C. E. Turner), while echoing the opinions of Dobrolyubov (1836–1861) and Pisarev (1841–1868) as to Turgenev's political position, stressed the novels as records of "the moral and philosophical movement in Russia". And the novel through which Turgenev became known to a wider public was *Virgin Soil*, which achieved its popularity mainly because of the publicity value of its theme. For in 1877, the very year of publication, the already widespread popular interest in the political unrest in Russia was suddenly heightened by news of the arrest and trial of a group of agitators—and a year later Vera Sassulich assassinated a prefect of police, and the famous "Trial of the hundred and ninety-three" followed. It was not surprising that *Virgin Soil* was read in the light of these events. Richard Littledale, for example, reviewing the book in the *Academy* (September 14th, 1878), treated it as a kind of political commentary rather than as a novel, describing it as "an account from the pen of an exceptionally shrewd and thoughtful writer, of the political condition of Russia, so far as it is affected at present by the secret societies which ramify in every direction . . ." and under these circumstances he felt that the value of the book was "beyond that of narrative and style", and it was not surprising to find Marianna described in *Blackwood's Edinburgh Magazine* as "the very stuff" of which Vera Sassuliches are made.

It would certainly be incorrect to dismiss the political aspects of Turgenev's work as irrelevant : he helped, as Zola had done, to drive home the lesson that the great social and political issues of the day could not be excluded from the field of serious fiction. But, unlike Zola and the Naturalists, he showed how it could be done without sacrifice of those moral and artistic values which the Victorians prized so highly, and without bringing the uglier facts of political strife too close.

Turgenev's politically conscious heroines certainly may have answered to the new ideas about the status of women, both in England and in America (where appraisals of Marianna's character sometimes led to comparisons with the feminist leader Mrs. Woodhall). But Marianna and Elena delighted just as much because they were high-spirited, idealistic girls of good country family, examples of what de Vogüé called "la jeune fille de province"—the very "corner-stone" he believed of Turgenev's scheme of values—who might without too violent a stretch of the imagination be placed side by side with, say, Dorothea in *Middlemarch*, or even Elizabeth in *Pride and Prejudice*.

As de Vogüé had argued, Turgenev showed "real life", but facts by themselves meant nothing to him : he looked at them only "through the human soul", and in their effect upon personality, and this was equally true of the political novels, such as *Virgin Soil* (which de Vogüé however placed below the others on "artistic" grounds), as of romances such as *A Nest of Gentlefolk* (1859). Indeed de Vogüé was representing his subject's own point of view with tolerable accuracy. Turgenev had, it is true, formulated (in 1852 in the Russian periodical the *Contemporary*) the theory of the novel as "a reflection of the elements of social life", but he had gone on in a second article to stress the importance of the novelist's concentration on his characters as human beings, and of his avoiding the temptation to overload "with unnecessary detail". And in his Introduction to the 1880 edition of his works he insisted that he had always tried "impartially and conscientiously to embody into types what Shakespeare called 'the body and the pressure of the time', and the swiftly changing physiognomy of the Russians of the educated classes who were mostly the objects of my observations". But the reservations in practice implied by the words "impartially and conscientiously" were, from the point of view of Turgenev's acceptance in nineteenth-century England, all-important. They stamped him as first and foremost an artist, not a politician.

In *A Sportsman's Sketches*, of course, Turgenev was not for the most part dealing with "Russians of the educated classes", and in many respects this, for the English, remained his most characteristic work. As we have seen, they believed that the book was directly instrumental in securing the liberation of the serfs. But there was nothing in this to antagonize English opinion. On the contrary, it corresponded to the liberal and humanitarian feeling of the day; the English had had their own "Abolitionist" movement, and reviewers were quick too to see the similarities between the conditions that had produced *A Sportsman's Sketches* and those which had inspired *Uncle Tom's Cabin*, though from the literary point of view the comparison was all in Turgenev's favour.

Turgenev's attitude towards his peasant characters, moreover, was tender and humane. He understood them better, sympathized with them more sincerely and was closer to them perhaps than any writer who had gone before—closer than Maria Edgeworth, for example, from whom he had learned so much. He did not rob them of their human dignity, and the influence of *A Sportsman's Sketches* undoubtedly helped to extend the boundaries, emotional and imaginative as well as social, of contemporary fiction. And undoubtedly he was "with them" and against both the spirit and the letter of autocracy.

But the sportsman whom we have seen so much in his element at the country house of Mr. Bullock Hall was also the landlord of Spasskoye. Between him and his serfs, whatever the mutual sympathy and good will, lay the gulf of class and breeding. Some critics have argued that it was he who initiated "the cult of the underdog" (the expression is Professor A. C. Ward's) which Gorky (i.e. Pyeshkov, 1868–1936) later elaborated, but there is no real continuity. Turgenev was the generous and philanthropic squire, who, gun under arm and dog at heel, wandered round his estate, watching with a kindly and observant eye the first green buds on the birch trees, the young birds hopping across the clearings and—with much the same gentle detachment—the human denizens of the scene. He could not enter into the intimate circumstances and into the souls of his peasant characters in the

D

way that Gorky or for that matter Chekhov, or even that other aristocrat Tolstoy, could. He was, to use Ford Madox Ford's phrase, "the rapt watcher", and a watcher is one who knows and keeps his distance. Turgenev was always and inescapably the patrician. As George Moore said, he

> "knew the serf as a gentleman knows the serf; he knew the gentleman as the gentleman knows the gentleman . . . While reading him we are always conscious of being in the company of a gentleman and a scholar—a scholar who has chosen to work in the novel, and who is putting into it the highest and best thought." (*Impressions and Opinions*, 1891).

To us, Moore's point of view seems a "snobbish" one, but it was, after all, an attitude inherent in the atmosphere of nineteenth-century England.

Turgenev was an aristocrat, however, of a pattern which the English of the mid-nineteenth century most appreciated and admired, an aristocrat with a good heart, a sense of duty, a proper appreciation of his place in society, and, at the same time, a social conscience. Something of a radical even, but a radical who could be trusted not to go too far. He seemed, in fact, not unlike his English counterparts among the benevolent Whig aristocrats of the day.

It was this fundamental patrician element in his make-up that made Turgenev suspect among the Russian revolutionaries of his own day, and among the "politically conscious" critics of the next generation, so that Brückner scoffed at him as "quite anachronistic", and Maurice Baring described him in 1909 as "one of those authors who powerfully affect one generation and are put on the shelf", as a man who had painted "an epoch that was already dead".

We are dealing, however, with a period when in spite of all the rapid changes, social, economic and political, and in spite of the spread of liberal and radical ideas throughout every section of the community, the English country house and the traditional values for which it stood were still unshaken, when there seemed no reason why country gentlemen, whose fathers had gone in for philanthropy, should not themselves be moved by progressive and enlightened ideas—and when the term "Social Democrat" had not even been invented. And it is this context that helps to give Turgenev his unique importance as "ambassador" and interpreter of the Russian Novel.

For the important point is that, at this particular juncture, none of the other Russian novelists could have performed the task. Tolstoy's opinions, though they were in fact politically far more "conservative" than Turgenev's (Tolstoy had little sympathy, for example, with the revolutionaries of his day, or even, at the outset, with the campaign for the liberation of the serfs), and Dostoyevsky's mystical, Slavophile brand of Conservatism, were, at any rate until the last decade of the century, still too unfamiliar and too intense for the contemporary climate of English opinion.

If, moreover, the majority of Turgenev's English admirers would have been hard put to it to understand the strictures of later critics such as Brückner, they would have been even more puzzled as to why a comparison with Tennyson (made by Brückner and others) should count as a point against Turgenev. The comparison would have delighted them because it pointed to a certain "Englishness" in Turgenev's attitude towards Nature—and it is interesting to note that Tennyson, who met the Russian on several occasions, admired him and was among the European men of letters who sent telegrams to him at the Pushkin celebrations in 1879.

For Turgenev's attitude towards Nature was, on the whole, thoroughly in accord with English tastes. As with Tennyson, many of his effects were derived from the background of the country house, from garden, parkland and meadow, from the villages that clustered around it, from the woods and coppices of the surrounding countryside. Nature in Turgenev (leaving aside the more grandiose reflections of the *Prose Poems*) is warmer, more intimate, more humanized and domestic than in most of the Russians, though S. T. Aksakov (1791–1859) is close to him in this respect. There is little of that sense of vast perspectives which we find in Tolstoy: the spaces of Russia figure little in his work, and when they do the focus of interest is usually some small group—as with the circle of boys round the campfire in "Byezhin Prairie" (one of the stories in *A Sportsman's Sketches*).

The first English article that dealt with the whole of Turgenev's fiction to date particularly noted the poetic atmosphere and the artistic economy in his descriptions of Nature, so very different from "the rude and coarse colouring" of the majority of Realistic novelists, and declared that Turgenev was "essentially a poet", who worked by "suggestiveness", "evoking" his characters and scenes "without laborious analysis or detail", and presenting Nature in her "softer and gentler manifestations" (the *British Quarterly Review*, 1869). Later on George Moore was to compare his landscape effects with those of Corot, and subsequent critics tended to follow his example—but this article shows that Turgenev's kind of "impressionism" was appreciated from the very beginning. Indeed his landscapes had not only the pastel shades, the tender, twilight effects, but also the exactness and clarity of the English water-colourists. He was not only interested in general effects and impressions. He was also a close observer—the "rapt watcher" who preferred, as he himself said in a letter to Pauline Viardot :

> "to contemplate the . . . movements of a duck's wet foot as it scratches the back of its head on the edge of a marsh, or the long and glistening drops of water slowly falling from the muzzle of a motionless cow which has just drunk at a pond in which she stands knee-deep, rather than all that the cherubim can behold in the sky".

He was not only a Corot, but also a kind of Russian Gilbert White : (in some respects too he reminds us of another Russian writer of the old tradition until recently living and writing in the new Russia—Michael Prishvin, the author of that beautiful book *The Lake and the Woods*). And it is this element in his work which has led to the comparisons between Turgenev and various English Nature writers—*A Sportsman's Sketches* has for example been likened to Richard Jefferies' *The Gamekeeper At Home*. Ford Madox Ford, too, saw Turgenev as a kind of Natural Historian of the human scene : he was, he wrote in *Thus to Revisit* (1921), an observer who "watched humanity with much such another engrossment" as W. H. Hudson watched kingfishers, sheep, or the grass of the fields, and "rendered his results with the same tranquillity"—an observer so "enamoured" that he himself "disappeared", having become "merely part of the surrounding atmosphere".

There were times, it is true, when Turgenev treated Nature as a distant, forbidding force, "indifferent, imperious, voracious, egoistic, pervading" (he wrote in one of the letters), "bringing forth a star as easily as it brings forth a pimple on the skin". And indeed Turgenev's "pessimism" constituted the only really serious flaw in his earlier reputation. It was the only point at which he seemed to come dangerously close to the "negative" philosophy of Flaubert and the French Naturalists. Thus the *Athenaeum* in 1863 complained of the "blank wan unhappiness" of his heroines. In 1880 *Blackwood's Edinburgh Magazine* thought that *Fathers and Children* was too tragic for English tastes, and even Henry James, the most ardent of all Turgenev's admirers, protested against his "wanton melancholy".

On the other hand the majority of these complaints were made more in sorrow than in anger. Most of the critics who advanced them were anxious to find excuses for Turgenev. In 1862, for example, the *Athenaeum* agreed that his preoccupation with "the happiest moment in life for the sudden burst of crushing and irrevocable doom" had a "Sophoclean element"; the *Saturday Review*, in 1881, in hailing Turgenev as "one of the greatest" European novelists, "acknowledged throughout Europe as reigning supreme", insisted that the total effect of his work was not really depressing, because its underlying "moral tone" preserved it from "the absolute negation" of the French Naturalists, rendering it "elevating and ennobling".

Most English readers in fact found that the presence of the moral element outweighed the pessimism, in which there were in any case elements that corresponded to an English tradition. The tone of some of his reflections—for example, in a letter dated July 16th, 1861 : "The small squeal of my consciousness . . . avails here as little as if I were childishly gabbling 'I, I, I', on the shore of an eternally moving ocean. The fly is still buzzing but in a moment it will cease—thirty or forty years is also a moment—and another fly . . . will begin to buzz, and so on for ever and ever."—puts one in mind of some of the animadversions of Sir Thomas Browne in *Religio Medici*. In other passages the sadness has a certain Stoic quality—of the type that many English gentlemen and scholars affected, even such devoutly Christian ones as Matthew Arnold. Turgenev's pessimism, moreover, was not, the English critics continually stressed, of the atheistic French type. His attitude towards religion was agnostic, liberal, humane.

"We also know, and very well too", George Moore wrote, "that we are with one who believes little in regeneration, who is convinced that we turn and turn in a circle, uttering little cries until overtaken by the great oblivion." But, he went on to emphasize,

> "he is not the ferocious cynic who, having drunk and found gall, would spit gall into every cup within reach; he is a man who, having learned the lesson throughly well, knowing we must live, since Nature has so willed it, is inclined towards kindness and pity; who would say 'Obey Nature's laws, be simple and obey; it is the best that you can do.' "

But much as Turgenev admired English literature, and some contemporary English writers, he could never have imagined that he "belonged" to the English—it was they who adopted him. "I am a European," he proclaimed, "and I love the banner, I pin my faith to the banner which I have carried since my youth."

It was, appropriately enough, in 1863, the very year that he quarrelled with Herzen because of his abjuration of "European" ideas in favour of Slavophilism, that Turgenev had been first introduced to the Flaubert group at the Restaurant Magny. From this time on he was a regular visitor to Flaubert's flat in the Faubourg St. Honoré, and when in 1874 Flaubert founded the famous "dinners of the hissed authors", Turgenev was one of the original select group to which besides himself and Flaubert only Zola, Edmund de Goncourt and Daudet were admitted.

His relations with the Naturalists both literary and personal were certainly close. He translated several of Flaubert's stories into Russian. He found a market for Zola, and indeed *La Faute de l'Abbé Mouret* made its first appearance in Russian (1874). He did the same for Maupassant, and he helped Merimée with his translations of *Smoke* and of several of the tales.

The French Realists, moreover, held him in the highest esteem and turned to him not only for practical help, but for encouragement and inspiration. Flaubert we know often consulted him on technical matters, placing the greatest value upon his judgment. "Depuis longtemps," he wrote, "vous êtes pour moi un maître" —and George Sand exclaimed when she read *The Living Relic* (in January 1874): "Maître! Nous devons aller tous à votre école!"

But what did Turgenev think of the French? Certainly he regarded himself as a Realist, whose vital concern was with "the truth", and in a letter to Sidney Jerrold, one of his English translators, he wrote (December 21st, 1882)—"Generally speaking, I always lean against the facts provided for me by life . . . merely trying as much as possible to raise accidental phenomena into types," and he was certainly not unaffected by the example of the French Realists.

The reservation about "accidental phenomena", however, the reluctance to hand over completely to them, as the Naturalists tended to do, was a significant one, and it was one he made frequently. Thus he wrote to Polonsky (1819–1898) in 1869: "Truth is the air without which we cannot breathe; but art is a plant which grows and develops in this air", and to another friend in 1874 he insisted "Realism by itself is fatal—truth, however powerful, is not art."

It was true too that he had a considerable respect for Flaubert (as well as a personal regard): *Madame Bovary* (1856–1857) he considered as "undoubtedly the most remarkable work of the new French school". But he had little real sympathy with any of the French novelists. Their approach seemed to him false in conception and practice. One has only to glance at a few of his numerous comments on the contemporary novel to see that the suggestion, which has been seriously advanced by some critics, that Turgenev was in reality a French author ("more French than the Parisian" James Huneker declared), a kind of junior partner in the Flaubert circle, is quite without foundation.

"Like the Romans whom they look upon as their predecessors the French are poorly endowed with poetic faculties," Turgenev wrote in 1869 in the Preface to a Russian translation of one of Du Camp's novels, for they "seem able to do without truth in art as easily as without freedom in social life". And in 1875 he told Saltykov-Schedrin (1826–1899) that in his opinion French writers were following the wrong path, that though they possessed great talent they "invented" too much—"Their literature stinks of literature, that's what's so bad."

His distrust of the French realistic technique went deep. He detested the "tremolo" of Hugo; the "sickly whining" of Lamartine; the chatter of "the garrulous old Sand" and the "cold obscenity" of Merimée. His disapproval reached back to Balzac whom he branded as "an ethnographer, not an artist". He provided, he wrote (in the Preface to another of Du Camp's novels, published in 1868),

> "an astounding example of a great talent existing in one and the same man side by side with a total incomprehension of artistic truth. . . . All his characters are so marvellously typical, they are so exquisitely worked out and finished to the last detail—and yet not one of them has ever lived, or indeed could have lived, and not one of them possesses even one particle of the truth which makes the characters of Tolstoy's *The Cossacks*,[1] for instance, so vitally alive."

The same inherent weakness, it seemed to him, undermined the work of Zola. *L'Assomoir* was appearing in the *République des Lettres* when George Moore first met Turgenev at a students' dance in Montmartre, and this quickly became a topic of conversation. Turgenev agreed that in Gervaise Zola had "for the first time . . . created a human being". But, he insisted, "the same vicious method" that pervaded all the French Realists was once again in evidence—"The desire to tell us what she felt" (in a purely physical, circumstantial sense) "rather than what she thought" (in an emotive, psychological sense). "Je me demande," he asked of George Moore, "qu'est ce que cela peut me faire si elle sue au milieu de dos ou sous ses bras?"

In other words Turgenev from the English point of view stood in a special relationship to the French. In a sense his presence in Paris heightened his efficacy as far as they were concerned. For he was close to the French, and he lived amongst them—but he was not one of them. He was a living protest against their "excesses", placed in their very midst. As Henry James pointed

[1] 1863.

out, Turgenev had "reservations and discriminations which set him apart". "The French capital," James insisted, "was an accident for him, not a necessity. It touched him at many points but it left him alone at many others."

It was exactly these "reservations and discriminations" which the English valued most highly. They explain for example the very real temperamental affinity that existed between the two guests of honour at that gathering at Six Mile Bottom in the Autumn of 1878. They were both aware of it, and they spoke of each other, as individuals and as writers, with affection and respect. Turgenev was, J. W. Cross tells us, "a very highly valued friend" of George Eliot (1819–1880) and he recalls that she used to say "that she had never met a literary man whose society she enjoyed so thoroughly and unrestrainedly as she did that of M. Tourguénieff". There were, he testifies, "innumerable bonds of sympathy" between them. This temperamental affinity can be seen best perhaps if we put side by side *A Sportsman's Sketches* and *Scenes of Clerical Life* (1857). There is the same choice of "anonymous" characters—the humble, the forgotten and the defeated, the same tenderness in their handling, and, especially in the love stories, the same play of sentiment, the same emotional spontaneity—and it must be admitted a similar proneness at times to sentimentality.

It would be possible to draw parallels between their ways of treating political themes and characters—as Henry James' comparison of Daniel Deronda and Insarov perhaps suggests. There are similarities in attitude and approach too between *Middlemarch* (1871–1872) and those novels of Turgenev's—*A Nest of Gentlefolk* itself for example, in which the struggles, aspirations, and ambitions of the mean-spirited and the generous are placed side by side in a carefully observed social milieu. Turgenev's women, too, in their independence of spirit, in their devotion to "duty", whether moral or emotional, often remind one of George Eliot's; and Lydgate's situation, tied to a vain and shallow wife, is not unlike that of Lavretsky in *A Nest of Gentlefolk*.

There is admittedly no evidence of influence as such but that is not the important point. George Eliot was in a very real sense representative of the whole English tradition, and de Vogüé had every justification in choosing her as the embodiment of those qualities which were most strongly opposed to the Naturalistic approach—and which lent themselves most readily to a comparison between English and Russian fiction.

The juxtaposition of George Eliot and Turgenev pointed therefore not only to the existence of that personal sympathy upon which writers depend for stimulation and encouragement, even if they exert no overt "influence" upon each other, and at the same time to the possibility that the Russian Novel in its turn might be absorbed into the great English tradition, just as the English Novel had been absorbed into the Russian. When in October 1866 Turgenev, at a time when he was known to only a handful of English readers, had written to his translator W. R. S. Ralston that the Russian novelists "ought to interest the English reader both because of their manner of perception and their transmission of poetic impressions"; he had in fact come close to anticipating de Vogüé's thesis, and his own special place in it. . . . The presence of the author of *A Sportsman's Sketches* and *A Nest of Gentlefolk* at the country house of Mr. Bullock Hall at Six Mile Bottom in Cambridgeshire "to compare English and Russian sport", is indeed one of the more pleasantly appropriate incidents of literary history.

CHAPTER FOUR

A NEST OF GENTLEFOLK AT CAMBRIDGE, MASSACHUSETTS

TURGENEV'S AMERICAN REPUTATION IN THE NINETEENTH CENTURY—HIS IMPACT ON THE YOUTHFUL HENRY JAMES

IF WE are looking for suitable backgrounds for Turgenev, however, the home of the James family, at Cambridge, Massachusetts, would serve almost as well as that of Mr. Bullock Hall in Cambridgeshire, England. For in 1874 Henry James the elder, not long after his son had written about Turgenev in the *Atlantic Monthly*, wrote to him at Carlsbad, inviting him to Cambridge, where his novels, he assured him, were so much admired, and so often discussed on the piazza, facing the New England sunset. And in his letter the would-be host envisaged his guest discoursing on the future of American civilization, in a haze of tobacco smoke—as evocative no doubt as that of the Autumnal bonfires at Six Mile Bottom.

The visit never took place, but a year after the invitation had been despatched to Turgenev, the younger Henry James himself crossed the Atlantic to seek him out in Paris.

But before we examine the implications of this meeting, it is necessary to look at some of the circumstances leading up to it. In the first place it is relevant to note that although he never set foot in the New World, Turgenev met quite a number of the Americans who came to the Old, and he surprised at least one of these, Hjalmar H. Boyesen, by his extensive knowledge of American literature.

One of the earliest meetings—with Harriet Beecher Stowe in 1856—is particularly interesting from the point of view of Turgenev's relationship with the American scene. This was four years after the publication of *Uncle Tom's Cabin* and two years after Charrière's translation of *A Sportsman's Sketches* had appeared in Paris (with the title *Mémoires d'un Seigneur Russe*).

The correspondence between the two books was quickly noted, in England as well as in America.

There were certainly some very obvious similarities between them. Harriet Beecher Stowe's book, like Turgenev's, was in effect a series of sketches. It was first published with the sub-title *Life Among the Lowly*; a further sub-title of one of the 1852 editions was *Pictures of Slavery in the United States of America*, and indeed in her Preface Harriet Beecher Stowe refers to it as a series of "sketches". There are, moreover, resemblances, not surprisingly perhaps, between the basic themes of the two books—lovers forcibly parted, children separated from parents at the whim of despotic owners, examples of heroism and dignity under suffering, occasional flashes of love and gaiety and so on.

These, however, are presumably the accident of time and circumstance, and there appears to be no evidence of literary "influence" (though Harriet Beecher Stowe, like Turgenev, may have had Maria Edgeworth's example in mind). But they do point to the existence of broad social and economic parallels between Russia and the Southern States of America, which undoubtedly helped to make Russian literature, and Turgenev in particular, more easily acceptable to American readers, and particularly of course to those of the Southern States.

Analogies between Russia and America were indeed something of a fashion in the last decades of the nineteenth century. Some of them were simple enough—obviously, for example, the two countries were comparable in their possession of vast territories still waiting to be opened up by the pioneer. It was argued that they were alike too in their rawness and youth: and that both were on the threshold of great destinies. Other comparisons were perhaps rather far-fetched—for example, that between the Russian *mir* and the New England town-meeting.

But these analogies undoubtedly had their effect upon the American reception of Turgenev and it was therefore not at all surprising that American writers should have found parallels between his characters and situations and those which they observed in the life around them—that the *Atlantic Monthly*, for example, should insist in 1877 that *Virgin Soil* was not "too Russian" because for every character in it could be found an American counterpart from "Anti-slavery or Fourierite, or

Woman Suffrage agitation", or that so many should have seen in Marianna a symbol of the New Woman of America.

Even Turgenev's Nihilists, it was found, could be interpreted in terms of the American scene. To sympathetic observers they appeared as the young and active agents of social change, with at least a distant relationship to the "go-getters" of the New America. To unsympathetic ones, on the other hand, they seemed to bear a resemblance to the more unpleasant, anti-social products of Civil War and its aftermath—and in addition of course there were the Nezhdanovs, the idealists who emerge—and suffer—in every period of transition.

In these circumstances Boyesen's prediction in 1874 that the United States would one day find an American Turgenev, who would produce "a grand, striking, and animated picture" of his native land, was not surprising. But to suggest that Henry James was the natural candidate for the rôle—that his relationship to Turgenev in other words must, in the first place, be considered in this social and political context, may perhaps strike some as surprising. We have become so accustomed to thinking of him in terms of his later work and the artistic and aesthetic pre-occupations that attended it, that we tend to overlook the effects that the pressure of the times had upon his creative imagination in its most fluid and impressionable stages.

That this is the correct "point of entry" into a consideration of James' earlier work however—and, at the outset, of Turgenev's impact upon it—is borne out by the reactions of contemporary critics. The evidence of the English periodicals of the '80s, surveying them both from a distance, is perhaps the most telling. Thus the *London Quarterly Review* asserted that it was the similarity between the Russian's Nihilists and the "carpet-baggers" of the post Civil War period in America that had made James "sympathetic" towards Turgenev, and *Blackwood's Edinburgh Magazine* was certain that although the American writer had "no such living source of agitation" as the Russian possessed, the "rabble of fine and vulgar Americans" who had "lately made irruption in fiction", were comparable to "the confused and fantastic society of the Russians". The writer has no hesitation in proclaiming the French version of Turgenev's *Smoke* as the "real inspiration of most of those clever and agreeable sketches by

Mr. Henry James, which have introduced so many elegant Americans to the English reader", and asserts that James' *Confidence* (1880) for the same reason "bears as much resemblance" to it "as a reflection in the water, slightly broken in outline and wavering in substance, does to the object reflected".

It was, however, the "similarity of the two nations *in their aspect abroad*"[1] to which *Blackwood's Edinburgh Magazine* particularly drew attention. The personal experience of expatriation indeed constituted an especially important bond. There are, of course, purely circumstantial reasons behind their presence in Europe—James' commissions to write travel sketches, for example, or more weightily, Turgenev's quarrels with the authorities. But they also went abroad because, in a more personal sense, they *had* to—that was their particular pattern of behaviour, as men and as artists, in face of the challenge of the times. From this circumstance, perhaps, spring other character-traits, Turgenev's morbidity and hypochondria for example, paralleled by James' increasing convolution of thought and style. There are cases, after all, where exile is not only a physical fact, but also a state of mind. James saw this clearly enough with reference to Turgenev, before he full realized perhaps that he was a similar case himself. In his first long article on Turgenev (published in the *North American Review* in April, 1874—a year before his own departure for Europe)—he described him as a writer "out of harmony with his native land", as "having what one might call a poet's quarrel with it"—which was indeed fundamentally James' own situation. "He loves the old," James goes on to say, "and he is unable to see where the new is drifting," words which provoke the heartfelt comment that American readers "will particularly appreciate this state of mind". For James argues (with specific reference to *Fathers and Children*) "the fermentation of social change" had "thrown to the surface in Russia a deluge of hollow pretensions and vicious presumptions, amid which the love either of old virtues or of new achievements finds very little gratification". And for an artist of a certain stamp, it may be extremely difficult to contemplate this particular kind of "social fermentation" at close quarters—and still remain an artist. It may inhibit the imagination instead of stimulating it and the only alternative

[1] My italics.

may be to withdraw, not indeed into a world of private fantasy, but to a distance at which the "old virtues" and "new achievements" can be seen in their proper perspective and a synthesis effected between them. The rôle of the observer, of the "rapt watcher", is not in fact only a habit or an artistic trick : it is also sometimes an artistic necessity.

As far as the novels are concerned there is of course the difference that Turgenev, except in *Smoke* (1867), went on writing about the "social fermentation" in the country he had left behind, whereas James dealt for the most part with expatriates like himself. But it would be a mistake to regard all the émigré Americans we meet in James pages merely as glorified globetrotters. They are not simply hunters after culture, fortune, marriage, or tourist diversions, even when they think they are. They too are products of the "social fermentation". This is true even of the rich and the leisurely, the pure and the innocent. Newman in *The American* (1876), for example, is one who has emerged, suddenly and triumphantly, from the maelstrom of expanding capitalism and cut-throat competition. And then there are all the wasters, and the spongers, the mothers with daughters to sell for cash or titles, the adventurers, gamblers, and speculators, with all their numerous hangers-on—all the flotsam and jetsam in fact of a society in a state of violent change—blown outwards like fragments from an erupting volcano.

James himself was in no doubt that in depicting his expatriate and cosmopolitan society he was dealing with "serious" social phenomena, and not merely producing facile "entertainment" (as he accused Trollope of doing), while in *The Princess Casamassima* (1890) it has been argued he made a more deliberate attempt to satisfy the promptings of his "social conscience". But again the concentration on the later work has led to an exaggerated emphasis on the "form" and "psychology" of the novels, taken in isolation. The fact is that in James the social and the moral, the psychological and the artistic factors are closely interrelated, and one would not exist without all the others. The juxtaposition of the social and the psychological, for example, is most aptly illustrated by James' description of Howells' women-characters as "delicate, nervous, emancipated young women, begotten of our institutions and our climate, and equipped with an irritable moral consciousness"—a diagnosis which could equally well be applied to many of James' characters, and certainly to his heroines.

Some consideration of these social factors therefore is an essential preliminary to any discussion of Turgenev's "influence" on Henry James. The bulk of any such discussion must, it is true, be in aesthetic or literary-critical terms, but it must proceed from the recognition of the underlying social elements : to do otherwise is to put the cart before the horse.

James' actual "discovery" of Turgenev, however, as a potent source of inspiration for his own creative work, as distinct from the premonitory recognition of fundamental sympathies (no doubt he had himself in mind when he suggested in the 1874 article that if America were ever to possess a "narrative novelist of a large pattern" he would probably approach the task as Turgenev did), was a slow and gradual process, keeping pace as it did with the long struggle to make the most satisfactory adaptation possible to the realities of his situation. And it is to this struggle that the "art" and the "aesthetics" belong. The whole process is in effect a forging of the instruments of creativity.

It is this indeed that makes the reading of James' criticism so exciting. For it is much more than an expression of opinions, or the application of objective "canons of criticism". It is also a passionate self-examination and self-preparation, a kind of public artistic purification. The various figures that come and go in the criticism, in the way of praise or of blame, must be seen in consequence as something very different from the chopping-blocks of the usual reviewer—they are figures in a creative drama, and each of them has an important part to play. They are "influences" in the genuinely creative sense of the term—that is they are symbolical of stages in an artist's growth and development ; they can be used, ruthlessly exploited—James had no false modesty about borrowing what he needed, or even imitating when imitation might teach him a new skill to add to his own resources. When in consequence they are cast aside, it is not out of pique, or boredom, or mechanical deference to changing fashions, but either because they have been thoroughly examined in the light of the creative need of the moment, and found wanting—or because the lessons they were able to teach have been absorbed and fresh nourishment is being sought. That is not to say, of course, that they have necessarily been condemned, or that the criticism is irresponsible, not of aesthetic value in itself: one artist takes from another what he needs, and that is sometimes the same thing as saying that he takes what he is able. An artist in his formative phases learns to know his own strengths and weaknesses, to understand when he is capable of doing better than his temporary model, and where he is unable, or does not want, to follow. But when eventually his mature work emerges the various "influences" have been as thoroughly absorbed as the vestiges of an ancient civilization, which can only be picked out from the air, have been absorbed in their surrounding terrain. There is no point, moreover, in picking them out unless they add to our understanding of the whole—which, no doubt, is why the study of the "influence of this upon that" can sometimes be such a futile proceeding.

In a writer such as James, to whom the world of books meant so much (to the impoverishment of 'real experience' some of his critics would say), the process is valuable and enlightening. He himself was in no doubt at all that it was "real life" that he was seeking to depict. "The air of reality" further defined as a certain "solidity of specification" was the quality above all others that he demanded of a novel. A novel was not worthy of the name if it did not represent real life; it succeeded only if it produced an illusion of reality which convinced us that, for the duration of that reality, we had "lived another life"—that we had undergone "a miraculous enlargement of experience". Life, not fantasy, was its province: "We care only for what is—we know nothing of what ought to be . . . the real is the most satisfactory thing in the world."

This belief was built into the very centre of his aesthetic system, and it always remained there. But its refining and defining was another matter, and through the early reviews we can see James, with reference to first one and then another practitioner of Realism, continually asking himself what he meant by the term. Thus by the time he came to consider Turgenev's example he had already cleared certain areas of his problem. In one of the early articles, for example, we can see him considering Scott's narrative verve, his "self-forgetfulness" in the dynamic flow of the plot, the pure "entertainment value" of

E

his work—and deciding that all these qualities were valuable (that is, were what he wanted for himself), at the same time that he is wondering whether they were sufficient (that is for his own creative purposes). A year later (in 1865), still debating what part exactly the "plot" must play in a novel, he draws, with reference to the two contemporary American women novelists whom he is reviewing, what clearly strikes him as a crucial distinction between "real" action—the inherent energy or motive force of a novel—and the mere accumulation of incident. With this discovery fresh in his mind we can see him finding much to admire in Trollope's narrative vitality, but denouncing him because he devoted himself to "the exhibition of circumstance" rather than to an "examination of motive", because he acted too much as a mere photographer, and made no attempt to get right into his "subject". And so emerge the first tentative gropings towards a conception of "character" in relation to "plot", which was later to become the corner-stone of his creative theory and practice.

We can see also his astonishment when he realizes that Goethe's *Wilhelm Meister* (in Carlyle's translation) can hold his interest, in spite of the fact that it has little real plot, little characterization, and little obvious "entertainment value"—because it is sustained by a lofty philosophical purpose. And we can see from his long review of *Felix Holt* (in 1866) that he is drawn towards George Eliot because she too possesses a genuine philosophic aim—and at the same time exhibits a "firm and deliberate delineation of individual character" and an "extensive human sympathy".

Our imaginary scene on the piazza of the James house in Cambridge, Massachusetts, would indeed need George Eliot's presence to make it complete, for his study of her methods is complementary to that of Turgenev's, and he often brings the two together, as by natural juxtaposition. At this stage, however, it is with George Sand that he makes his comparison, deciding that though the Englishwoman is right to make character the "tone" of her novels, her plots have "too many loose ends": that the Frenchwoman, on the other hand, possesses a wonderful "fluency" (a quality he was to envy her all his life), but that she was too fond of moral ugliness; that George Eliot's study of the workings of the conscience was admirable, but that conscience, on the other hand, was an inadequate substitute for passion.

We can see him, too, with his own determination to become an interpreter of the American scene always at the back of his mind, examining the work of other American novelists, realizing, for example, from the case of Hawthorne, that it was possible for an American to be an artist, "one of the finest", without going outside America, but at the same time deciding that Hawthorne's blend of realism and symbolical fantasy was not for him. At the same time, however, we can see him realizing under the influence of his friend and contemporary William Dean Howells, that his conception of reality and truth could also include "romance". We can trace the first stages of his discipleship to Balzac, perhaps the greatest single influence of his earlier years, and one he never entirely abandoned, observing his admiration for Balzac's breadth of canvas and vitality of characterization—the way in which, above all, he gets down to the task of activating his story without fuss or clumsy machinery. And finally we can see him turning to a consideration of a kind of realist different from any of these— the Russian Turgenev.

This was not surprising, for, as we have seen, Turgenev already had his select band of American admirers. The three leading "highbrow" American periodicals during the years of James' apprenticeship—the *North American Review*, the *Nation*, and above all the *Atlantic Monthly* under the editorship of William Dean Howells, were professedly concerned with "the art of fiction" and Turgenev was soon brought into this context.

I. S. Perry, for example, although he was dubious about *Virgin Soil*—feeling that Turgenev had attempted to harness together "two uncongenial horses, information and entertainment"—praised his technique of characterization, whereby rather than dissect them he made his people *show* themselves, and described him as "a realist in the sense of hiding himself". Similarly G. P. Lathrop stressed Turgenev's "self-renunciation", forecasting that it would have a "general and far-reaching influence", and contrasting this essentially "dramatic" technique with the theatrical methods of the usual run of novelists. These were ideas which found a receptive listener in Henry James.

As for Howells, in *My Literary Passions* (1895) he recalled "the joyful astonishment", the "rapture inexpressible", with which he first read Turgenev:

"I cannot describe the satisfaction his work gave me," he wrote; "I can only impart some sense of it perhaps by saying that it was like a happiness I had been waiting for all my life, and now it had come I was richly content for ever."

To Howells the example of a novel such as *Dmitri Rudin* (1856) seemed to provide a perfect challenge to the "sickly literary taste" of the times. It was so on moral grounds as much as on technical.

"Life showed itself to me in different colours," he wrote, "after I had once read Turgenev; it became more serious, more awful, and with mystical responsibilities I had not known before. My gay American horizons were bathed in the vast melancholy of the slow, patient, trustful agnostic. . . ."

He marvelled, too, at the way in which Turgenev's technique sprang, not from a mere decision to manipulate this device or that, but from the inherent *moral* necessity of the story. He never called upon his readers to "admire how well he does a thing; he only makes you wonder at the truth and value of the thing, when it is done", he wrote in the *Atlantic Monthly* (February 1873).

This kind of effect, however, Howells agreed with Perry and Lathrop, could be achieved only when an author resisted the temptation to add his own comment, providing only what was necessary for the reader's intelligence, and rigorously excluding all superfluities: otherwise a novel must sink to the level of a "panorama" and the novelist become a mere showman picking out the interesting points with his long stick.

The fact that a fellow novelist whom he respects has been able to discover in the Russian novelist such fruitful precepts is naturally of importance to James. Some of these precepts appear in his first article on Turgenev—a review of the German translation of *A Lear of the Steppes* (1870) and *The Torrents of Spring* (1872) published in the *North American Review* for April 1874. It provides the occasion for a serious sorting out of his ideas, both those he has taken from his contemporaries and those he has discovered for himself, perhaps the most momentous that he has hitherto undertaken, for in the course of it he finds that his doubts about the French Realists have considerably deepened.

He finds that Turgenev belongs to "the limited class of very careful writers", and he is inclined to regret that with his "line of narrow observation" he is a "zealous" rather than an "abundant" genius. In this he lacked "the faculty of rapid, passionate, almost reckless inventiveness" that he had found in Scott and Dickens, in George Sand and Balzac. On the other hand he sees that Turgenev's "narrowness" has valuable compensations. His constant concern to be what Howells called a "dramatic" novelist meant that "abstract possibilities" were immediately translated into "concrete situations". He was a poet who never played the chorus to his own characters : his situations spoke for themselves, and so did his characters.

And although he still hankers after the fluency and passion of George Sand, and the richly populated canvases of Balzac, he now sees that Turgenev's method too makes for "the air of reality" and the "certain solidity of specification". He comes to the conclusion, in fact, that Turgenev is greater even than Balzac, because he was less of a "showman" ; he certainly did not, stick in hand, present a mere panorama. It was he, even more than Balzac, who displayed every degree of fortune, every type of character, every class of society, every phase of manners, for he "had an eye for all our passions, and a deeply sympathetic sense of the wonderful complexity of our souls". He is beginning to see, moreover, that Turgenev's apparently artless method is genuinely Realistic, at the same time that it serves a serious and truly "moral" purpose. And it is here that we can see the beginning of the drawing together of morality and aesthetics—the dawning of the realization that the form and the purpose should interpenetrate each other. Thus he discovers in *A Sportsman's Sketches* "a capital example of moral meaning giving a sense to form, and form giving relief to moral meaning"—whereas the French Realists have more often than not created "little vases, skilfully moulded and chiselled, into which unclean things have been dropped". Turgenev, in fact, possesses "an apprehension both of man's religious impulses" and of "the aesthetic passion" and he closely mingles Realism and

Idealism. If his manner is that of a "searching realist" his temper is that of a "devoutly attentive" observer, and this made his view of the great spectacle of human life "more genial, more impartial, more unreservedly intelligent than that of any novelist we know" —except perhaps George Eliot.

For there is one respect in which Turgenev has, so far, failed to win his confidence: the great question about a poet or a novelist, he has come to believe, is "How does he feel about life? What, in the last analysis, is his philosophy?" And here, James regretfully decides, even Turgenev's "seriousness" is suspect: it is too morbid: he takes "life hard, terribly hard", and in consequence his work is not "altogether purged of sarcasm". It is for this reason that James finds, at this stage in his development, that in spite of the looseness of her plots, in spite of her stifling of passion and the intrusion of an over-Puritanical conscience, George Eliot must still challenge Turgenev for first place in his affections. Her presence, as well as his, haunts the piazza of the James house in Cambridge, Massachusetts.

CHAPTER FIVE

THE BEAUTIFUL GENIUS

TURGENEV'S INFLUENCE IN THE NOVELS
AND SHORT STORIES OF HENRY JAMES

ALL this time James was doing his best to practise what he preached. In the earliest stories we can see him desperately striving to reconcile the claims of plot, character, fluency, passion, conscience, morality. Which of these elements would come to the top? *Roderick Hudson* which he began in Florence in the Spring of 1874, and which was published serially in the *Atlantic Monthly* during 1875, gave the answer.

Certainly the French influences are still there, but the dominant one is that of Turgenev. Even Christina Light, who is in many respects a *femme fatale* of the George Sand type, owes something to him. The contradictions in her nature, the unhappiness beneath the superficial gaiety, the desire to dazzle and the haunting fear of a fundamental inability to feel, all remind one (at the moment we are speaking at the simple level of "reminders") of Madame Odintsov in *Fathers and Children*. Christina's mother, too, "reminds" one of Marya Dmietrevna Kalitin in *A Nest of Gentlefolk*, who is a kind of prototype of many of those mothers in James who are, to use Turgenev's phrase, "more sentimental than kind-hearted".

Madame Grandoni, again, "reminds" one of Marfa Timofyevna in the same novel—and undoubtedly there is a certain similarity between Turgenev and the early James in the motivations and the groupings of the minor characters. In Mary Garland, too, we see James' first real attempt at the creation of a type of womanhood which bears, at the least, a strong general resemblance, physical as well as psychological, to many of Turgenev's heroines—many of whom possess, to quote James' apt description, "the faintly acrid perfume of the New England temperament" together with a "hint of Puritan angularity".

Mary Garland, and many of her successors—Catherine

71

Morland in *Washington Square* (1881) for example—fit into this formula. They have the same kind of looks, the same deportment, even the same grey-blue eyes. In the case of Turgenev's heroines of course the plainness of feature is made beautiful by the warmth of personality, and the spiritual glow within, and in his revisions of *Roderick Hudson* James, aware that Mary was insufficiently "realized", attempted to give her something of this inner charm.

If one's ears are attuned to the two authors, it is also possible to detect situations in *Roderick Hudson* which echo some of those which he had recently been reading in Turgenev's novels. The outing arranged by Anna Vassilyevna in *On the Eve* (1860) for example puts one in mind of that in James' novel. Several of the passages describing Roderick's experiences at Baden-Baden are similar in tone, intention and style to scenes in *Smoke*, as, for example, when Roderick meets various "gentlemen with wonderful names, polyglot ambrosial gentlemen who walked about in clouds of fragrance, called him 'mon cher', sat at roulette all night and supped the next morning" and whom he had at first "found himself in the mood for thinking . . . types of a high, if somewhat spent civilization".

And when we read about Rowland Mallet as he "sat beside his companion and looked away at the far-spreading view, which affected him as melting for them both into such vast continuities and possibilities of possession. It touched him to the heart; suddenly a strange feeling of prospective regret took possession of him", it is difficult not to remember those golden but poignant scenes in Turgenev in which young friends sit in the sunshine wrapped in moods of mingled happiness and "prospective regret" —Bazarov and Arkady, for example, under the haystack, or Bersenyev and Shubin "On one of the hottest days of the summer of 1853" lying "in the shade of a tall lime-tree, on the bank of the river Moskva". . . .

Shubin is, in fact, important from our point of view. He is, of course, only a minor character in *On the Eve*, and with his childish tantrums he is a more conventional portrait of the "artistic temperament" than Roderick. But in some respects the two are remarkably alike. Turgenev's sculptor, like James', has a wealthy patron: and Shubin's patron, like Roderick's, discovers his "youthful genius" by unexpectedly coming across an example of his work during a visit to a relative. And even the kinds of work they do have a certain similarity: Shubin's bas-relief of the boy with the goat, for example, reminds one of Roderick's first sculpture, which catches the eye of Rowland Mallet. But what is far more interesting is the similarity in their attitude towards their work, and in the fitful nature of their inspiration—potentially tragic in Shubin's case, actively so in Roderick's. Shubin, like Roderick, shows the unmistakable signs of genius, but like Roderick he is prevented from fulfilling them by the weakness of his character, of which, like Roderick, he is only too bitterly aware.

"What strikes me most forcibly in the ants and grass-hoppers and other worthy insects," Shubin says to Bersenyev, as they lie beside the river Moskva, "is their astounding seriousness. They run to and fro with such solemn air as though their life was something of such importance! A man, the lord of creation, the highest being, stares at them, if you please, and they pay no attention to him!"

Through much of this chatter of Shubin's runs an undertone of spitefulness and irony, as through Roderick's apparent flippancies. The flippancy of both, in fact, springs from the same realization of inherent failure and defeat. When, for example, Bersenyev questions Shubin about his progress he bursts out:

"Hang it! Hang it! Hang it! . . . I looked at the genuine old things, the antiques, and I smashed my rubbish to pieces. You point to Nature and say 'There's beauty here too.' Of course there's beauty in everything, even in your nose there's beauty, but you can't toy after all kinds of beauty. The ancients, they didn't toy after it; beauty comes down of itself upon their creations from somewhere or other—from heaven I suppose. The whole world belonged to them, it's not for us to be so large in our reach; our arms are short. We drop our hook into one little pool, and keep watch over it. If we get a bite, so much the better, if not . . ."

This is the very tone of Roderick's inner despair. Like Shubin, Roderick finds that he is eventually reduced to dropping his hook into a little pool, and like Shubin he reaches a state in which he doubts if he will ever draw anything out of it again. As artists both are fundamentally disorientated, out of touch with the springs of their creativity: they can "see, not feel" how beautiful the world around them is. And when Bersenyev says to his friend: "You will go to Italy . . . and will do nothing. You will always be pluming your wings and never take flight. We know you!" it might be a more far-sighted Rowland Mallet speaking to a Roderick in whom he has, at the very first meeting, detected the seeds of failure. It also seems likely that the two busts of Insarov which Shubin makes—the one genuine, the other a cruel caricature to satisfy his hatred and jealousy—suggested Gloriani, the Italian sculptor, who is a kind of satirical chorus to Roderick, and who avoids Roderick's dilemma by deliberately setting out to model only ugly things.

Shubin, however, is only a sketch: Dmitri Rudin is a finished portrait, and it is his influence that is undoubtedly the fundamental one—both in *Roderick Hudson* and from the point of view of James' later development. For as the 1874 article shows, James has seen that though Turgenev had a passion for shifting his "point of view" (a passion which he was to share) his object was always the same—"that of finding an incident, a person, a situation" which would be "morally interesting". And he saw too that what above all *made* a character morally interesting was failure. Thus Dmitri Rudin was

"a moral failure, like many of the author's heroes—one of those fatally complex natures, who cost their friends so many pleasures and pains; who might, and yet evidently might not, do great things; natures strong in impulse, in talk, in responsive emotion, but weak in will, in action, in the power to feel and do singly".

This was Roderick's character too, and other studies of subjects that were "morally interesting" were to follow.

.   .   .   .   .

It was the journey to Europe in 1875 that marked the climax of James' apprenticeship. It was of course by no means the first, but previously his main concern had been to absorb European sights and sounds, to soak himself in European traditions and culture, to take home what he had learned and then to try and settle down to observe the American scene, still believing that it was here that his destiny as a novelist lay. But when he set out for Europe in the Autumn of 1875 it was in quite a different frame of mind, as Howells obviously guessed when he wrote to a friend "Harry James is gone abroad again, not to return, I fancy, even for visits." It was indeed the beginning of his exile, that exile which was in effect a recognition, though not yet clearly formulated, of the conditions that alone would further the growth of his genius. He had begun to realize that his youthful ambition to become "the American Balzac" was an unreal one, that when he set out to depict the American scene, he generally failed, that it was his studies of the American abroad that came nearest to the true "air of reality", the genuine "solidity of specification".

This increasing awareness of the true field of his endeavour coincided with a growing realization that his earlier masters were no longer to his purpose. He came to Paris determined to sort out his ideas, once and for all, to resolve past doubts and inconsistencies, and to complete the last stage in his self-preparation.

A good deal has been written about this year in France, and it has been suggested that the real reason for his rejection of the French Realists was some affront which he imagined he had suffered at their hands. It may be true that there was some such personal hurt—it may, for example, have lain behind his sympathy for Newman in *The American*—but it is beside the point. The misgivings were already there, the shift of emphasis had already started—and was indeed inherent even in his earliest critical writings. And, as we have seen, his reorientation towards the example of Turgenev had started before he left home.

Nevertheless he was genuinely excited to find himself living in Paris, to be meeting his old heroes face to face. He could still write: ". . . There is nothing more interesting to me now than the effort and the experiment of their little group. . . . They do the only kind of work to-day that I respect. . . ."

But it was not long before his disillusionment had become almost complete. His previous misgivings on the score of morality were confirmed absolutely. Flaubert was further attacked;

Madame Bovary, L'Éducation Sentimentale (1869), *Salammbo* (1862) were all condemned as fundamentally "unpleasant", as a waste of talent, an abuse of art. The Goncourts were described as exhibiting a typically Parisian culture, "very exquisite" of its kind, but essentially contrived—"a studio question, as it were". Their concern for the "picturesque" in Realism (which usually meant the "unclean") had "somehow killed the spiritual sense" : the moral side of the work was "dry and thin".

Even Balzac's stature suffered considerable diminution in the article contributed to *Galaxy* in the December of 1875. He was presented indeed as a great novelist, behind whose characters was "a certain heroic pressure" : his imagination was working at great heat : it was pictorially vast, sturdy, and systematic. But he no longer appeared to James as the "ideal historian" he had once thought him. He was reduced to the status of a "realistic romancer", who had failed in the portrayal of "superior" intellectual virtue.

George Sand too, was judged and found wanting. When in 1877 he came to write an obituary article for *Galaxy* he was embarrassed to find that he could not summon up his old enthusiasm. She no longer seemed to him a real creator—she was merely an "improvisatrice". Her apparent philosophizing, in her long analytical passages, was fundamentally false. Even the emotional vigour he had once so much admired was now revealed as a sham—she might illuminate "the divine passion", he wrote, but she also "cheapened" it—she let it "so little alone".

In the course of this process of readjustment, moreover, James arrived at a clearer and more subtle understanding of what he meant by morality in fiction. It was, he argued in a review of Baudelaire's *Les Fleurs du Mal*, not a matter of mere prudery but an integral part of life, and to deny its existence was "ineffably puerile". To leave out the moral element in one's appreciation of an artistic total would be no more sensible than (in the case of a poem) to leave out all the words of three syllables or "to consider only such portions of it as were written by candlelight". Morality was not something kept in a bottle, to be sprinkled in or left out according to the whim of the artist. It was rather "a part of the essential richness of inspiration". It had nothing to do with the artistic process—but it had everything to do with the artistic effect, and the more a work of art felt its influence at its roots, the richer it would be. In other words the artistic and the moral were in a sense coterminous, in so far as a fine moral fibre produced work of a fine artistic fibre.

And as his ideas about the French Realists gradually came to a head, so inevitably did those about the two writers whom he had already recognized as their natural rivals. For in George Eliot and Turgenev were examples of novelists in whom the moral element was indeed inherent, working at the "very source of their inspiration".

When, James declared in the essay on Balzac, we entered into the world created by these writers, we had the sense of entering into "great consciences and great minds", whereas with Balzac it was a case of entering into "a great temperament, a prodigious nature", with, alas, "no natural fancy of morality". And in his review of *Terres Vierges* (in the *Nation*, April 26th, 1877) he proclaimed Turgenev and George Eliot as the only living novelists the publication of whose works could be considered as genuine "literary events".

His admiration for George Eliot remained, and she must always be present in any consideration of the influence of Turgenev on Henry James. But during these vital years in Europe, he finally adjudicated between them. He realized, as he read *Daniel Deronda*, which was appearing in monthly instalments during 1876, that in her case the art and the morality were *not* coterminous. There was no novelist with a profounder understanding of the part that duty and conscience must play in human affairs : but these elements, it now came home to him, were not properly fused with the other elements of plot, situation, style, in order to make a single whole.

Only in Turgenev, in fact, was this synthesis, which he was now convinced was the real aim of the serious novelist—*his* aim —satisfactorily accomplished. In George Eliot there was too much of the set thesis : Insarov in *On the Eve*, for example, was created as a real man who stood upon his own feet within the space of two hundred pages (though other critics have seen Insarov as the least satisfactory of Turgenev's heroes) whereas George Eliot expended eight hundred upon Daniel Deronda, and with far less success. Turgenev, moreover, did not "stifle" passion as George Eliot tended to do: he gave it free play—and yet managed to bring it into contact with conscience.

In a later essay on George Eliot (1885) James pushed these conclusions a stage further, deciding that the great fault in her work was that it was not "primarily a picture of life, capable of deriving a high value from its form", but a moralized fable, "the last word of a philosophy endeavouring to teach by example". *Romola* (1863), for example, "smelt of the lamp", it tasted "just perceptibly of pedantry". Her great weakness was "the absence of free aesthetic life".

The absence of "free aesthetic life" was certainly the last fault, James might have said, that one could urge against Turgenev. On all counts, in fact, he emerged as the best of all contemporary novelists, as the one most worthy to command the admiration and respect of a young novelist who was determined to be satisfied with nothing but the best.

Of all the writers whom James came to Paris to meet in 1875, therefore, Turgenev was the only one who did not disappoint him, either as a writer or as a man. It was indeed Turgenev who introduced him to the Flaubert circle, but by May of the following year we find him writing to Howells ". . . there are fifty reasons why I should not become intimate with them. I don't like their wares, and they don't like any others; and besides they are not *accueillants*. Turgenev is worth the whole heap of them . . ." and in a letter to his brother, dated July 1876, he wrote ". . . my last layers of resistance to a long encroaching weariness and satiety with the French mind and its utterances have fallen from me like a garment". It was not long in fact before he came to prefer the gatherings at Mme Viardot's to those in Flaubert's apartment— but better still were the precious "talks à deux" in Turgenev's "little green sitting room", or in his library at Bougival, or (in recollection most poignant of all) "the long noonday breakfasts" in "dusky cafés". "There are places in Paris," he wrote years later, "which I can think of only in relation to some occasion on which he was present."

It was not surprising, therefore, that Turgenev's influence, absorbed not merely as a "literary example", but also as the emanation of a real and affectionate human relationship, should continue to affect his work. It is apparent indeed in many of the shorter pieces that followed *Roderick Hudson*. *Four Meetings*, for example (*Scribner's Magazine*, November 1877), bears an obvious resemblance to Turgenev's *Three Meetings*: both stories are related by a detached onlooker, who sees his "subject" only in the light of random flashes provided by a series of accidental meetings, and who, as a complete stranger, is powerless to help.

It is obvious too that *Daisy Miller* (first published in the *Cornhill Magazine*, June–July 1878) has points in common with some of Turgenev's heroines; Daisy reminds us of James' own description of them in his 1874 article—as creatures whose "spontaneity and independence" are "quite alien to the English ideal of maiden loveliness". Some contemporary critics found fault with the technique of *Daisy Miller* on the grounds that it was a series of "photographs": far more suggestive are the words James himself had applied to Turgenev—"he is a story-teller who has taken notes" ... whose tales are " 'magazines' of small facts, of anecdotes and of descriptive traits, taken ... 'sur le vif' ". This is indeed the method of the story, and Daisy herself certainly creates the impression that she has been taken "sur le vif". The influence of the French writers can still be detected, it is true, both in these tales and in James' next novel—*The American*: the whole business of the Bellegardes' "sinister secret", for example, is pure George Sand melodrama. But it is Turgenev's presence which permeates it. The main concern is again with a character who is "morally interesting", and made more so by failure. Not this time by reason of his own weakness; as James had pointed out in his first article on Turgenev, the failure can spring either from a flaw of character, as in the case of Dmitri Rudin, or from the force of external circumstances as in the case of Lavretsky. Newman, like Lavretsky, is a "strong" character: the tragedy of each is brought about not by any moral defect but by the machinations of people of a coarser fibre: the group ranged against Lavretsky—his wife Varvara Pavlovna, Lisa's mother, Marya Dmietrevna, the careerist fop Panshin, is paralleled by the Bellegardes and their hangers-on.

It is indeed *A Nest of Gentlefolk* more than any other of Turgenev's novels that lies behind *The American*. In his 1874 article, he had already noted, with reference to this novel, that "a pair of lovers accepting adversity" seemed to Turgenev "more eloquent than a pair of lovers grasping at happiness". The formula sums up perfectly the situation of Newman and Claire in *The American*. There are indeed superficial resemblances even in the ordering of the respective lovers' fates in the two books: thus Claire, like Lisa, enters a convent, when her romance has been cruelly destroyed, and Newman, like Lavretsky, visits the convent walls for a mute farewell (though unlike Lavretsky Newman does not get a last glimpse of his beloved). And in both novels, of course, the main protagonists, in spite of their personal tragedies, emerge as the moral victors with their integrity intact.

The conclusions of the two novels are indeed so alike that several of the English and American reviews of James' novel rapped him over the knuckles for deliberately imitating Turgenev. But the superficial resemblances are of importance only in so far as they reflect the crystallizing of his ideas about Realism into this fundamental conviction—that the pivot of a novel must be in a character who is "morally interesting", that it is from this premise that the novelist must always begin, and that the novelist's task is then to precipitate his characters into the situations that will best reveal their moral qualities—that will, in other words, most freely allow them to be *themselves*.

In the article which he wrote in 1884 soon after Turgenev's death he pointed out that "the germ of a story with him was never an affair of plot—that was the last thing he thought of : it was the representation of certain persons" ; that the very first form "in which a tale appeared to him was as the figure of an individual, or a combination of individuals, whom he wished to see in action".

The choice of the central character was one thing, however ; to make him stand up definite and vivid, to make him *show* himself in the right kind of actions, the right kind of situations, was another. The starting-point of *The American* was, as James said in the Preface to the later edition, the "figure of an individual" whom he wished to see in action, the "happy halting view of an interesting case". Newman's character and the way such a character would react when the opportunity of revenge was placed into his hands "constituted in fact the subject". Had he, however, really succeeded in this perfect integration of character and plot ?

In Turgenev "the thing consists", James wrote in his 1884 article, "of the motions of a group of selected creatures which are not the result of preconceived action, but a consequence of the qualities of the action". But Newman, James came to suspect, *was* too much the issue of a "preconceived action". Would Newman, in fact, have *behaved* in quite that way—was the "fashion of coming about" really appropriate to his particular case? Or was it that he had not, as Turgenev had recommended, studied his central character carefully enough, built up his "dossier" with sufficient thoroughness? Had he formulated with sufficient clarity that basic challenge which Turgenev always put to himself—"What shall I make my characters *do* that will show them completely?"

With his next novel he had no such doubts. *The Portrait of A Lady* (1881) marks the climax of this phase of James' development, and it is the novel in which he arrived at his full maturity. The picking out of superficial similarities in plot and characterization to this writer or that becomes now, as with all great writers who have "won through" to the sources, unique and utterly private, of their own creative imagination, of very minor importance. It is not necessary, therefore, at the level of the obvious "influences" to enter into great detail. It is certainly appropriate that most of these derive from Turgenev and George Eliot. James' earlier admiration of the French Realists still makes itself felt—but the portrait of Madame Merle, to take the obvious example, owes no more to George Sand's than it does to Turgenev's more complex and ambiguous version of the *femme fatale*, while Gilbert Osmond is predominantly a Panshin-type character.

Isabel Archer clearly owes nothing whatsoever to George Sand, though she undoubtedly does bear a family relationship to the heroines of Turgenev and George Eliot. What James had said about Gwendolen Harleth in *Daniel Deronda* might in many respects be applied to Isabel:

"Gwendolen is a perfect picture of youthfulness—its eagerness, its presumption, its preoccupation with itself, its vanity, its silliness, its sense of its own absoluteness. But she is extremely intelligent and clever, and therefore tragedy *can* have a hold upon her. Her conscience doesn't make the

F

tragedy, it is the tragedy which makes her conscience, which then reacts upon it."

In Turgenev's portrait of Elena in *On the Eve* too, we can sense a kinship:

"She was tall, and had a pale, dark face, large grey eyes under arching brows, covered with tiny freckles, a perfectly regular forehead and nose, tightly compressed lips, and a rather sharp chin. Her hair, a chestnut shade, fell low on her slender neck. In her whole personality, in the expression of her face, intent and a little timorous, in her clear but changing glance, in her smile which was, as it were, intent . . . in her soft and uneven voice, there was something nervous, electric, something impulsive and hurried. All impressions cut deeply into her heart ; life was bitter earnest for her."

Isabel, of course, has in her make-up less of that Puritan angularity, which James had noted in Turgenev's Marianna, and more of the warmth and tenderness of Lisa, but her integrity and steadfastness is equal to theirs, and she might well have echoed Sophia's words in Turgenev's short story *Yakov Pasynkov* (1855) —"Our life is not in our hands, but we all have one anchor, from which one can never, without one's own will, be torn—a sense of duty."

The construction of the novel, again, bears a relationship to Turgenev's methods. Both writers work towards one central emotional and moral crisis. And this climax, though it is brought about by external circumstances, the events in the "story", takes place deep in the souls of the main protagonists. Just as in *A Nest of Gentlefolk* or in *On the Eve*, the threads are suddenly drawn closer at the point when they are brought face to face with their personal, and fundamentally lonely crisis, so the whole of *The Portrait of A Lady* turns upon Isabel's "extraordinary meditative vigil" as James called it in his Preface—the "vigil of searching criticism" which throws the action "further forward than twenty incidents might have done".

But all this is merely to say that in *The Portrait of A Lady* James *had* achieved his purpose. He was no longer dependent, as

in *The American*, upon such contrivances as guilty family secrets
and incriminating letters. Isabel's "extraordinary meditative vigil"
was evidence of a character absolutely realized and of "plot"
completely integrated with "character"—for if the novel *was* the
character, where else but in the consciousness of its main pro-
tagonist *could* the climax lie?

He had in fact absorbed Turgenev's lessons at a far deeper
level than that where superficial resemblances count, and the
evidence for his influence is not now a matter of trying to isolate
them, or of looking for hints in reviews and articles—but of
examining James' own professions of indebtedness. For now
there was no need for him to make any bones about it.

Thus in the Preface to the 1907 edition of *The Portrait of
A Lady* he recalls a remark of Turgenev's which he had "always
fondly remembered", about the true origin of "the fictive picture":

> "It began with him," James wrote, "almost always with
> the vision of some person or persons who hovered before him,
> soliciting him, as the active or passive figure, interesting him
> and appealing to him just as they were and by what they were."

Turgenev saw them, he told James, as "*disponibles*", creatures
already vividly conceived, but still awaiting the "right relations"
to "bring them out". And to arrive at these "right relations",
Turgenev had continued, one only had to look at one's characters
long enough and one would see them come together, one would
see them "placed"—"engaged in this act and in this or that
difficulty", and the novel would in effect consist of an account of
how they would look and move and speak and behave in the
"setting" in which the novelist had placed them.

For his own part, James tells us, the "germ" of his idea too
in *The Portrait of A Lady* "consisted not at all in any conceit of
a 'plot', nefarious name . . . but altogether in the sense of a single
character, the character of a particular engaging young woman".
He had started, in fact, as Turgenev would have recommended,
from Isabel Archer, as she stood before his eyes "in perfect
isolation". He had wondered for a moment "by what process of
logical accretion" this "mere slim shade of an intelligent but
presumptuous girl" could possibly find herself "endowed with the

high attribute of a subject?" And the answer had been, as once again Turgenev would have recommended, to place the "centre of the subject in the young woman's consciousness" and to let the minor characters gather around it. For these were merely "the numbered pieces" of the puzzle, "the concrete terms" of the plot, and they had all floated into his mind without difficulty in response to the primary question: "Well what will *she* do?"

By the time he came to write the Preface to *The Portrait of A Lady* James was able to look back on these conversations with Turgenev from the vantage point of his own maturity, as a fellow artist, rather than as a callow young disciple, and even to congratulate himself on having written a novel with more "architecture" to it than Turgenev could command. But he can still recall "with comfort" the "gratitude" with which he welcomed Turgenev's "reference to the intensity of suggestion that may reside in the stray figure, the unattached character, the image *en disponibilité*". It gave him, he confesses, "a higher warrant" than anything else he had hitherto encountered. He had, he admits, still tended to look with envy on the writer who was so constituted that he could "see his fable first" and "make out its agents afterwards". But Turgenev had shown him that this approach was neither necessary nor sound.

And after this it was "impossible" for him not to read "high lucidity into the tormented and disfigured and bemuddled questions of the objective value, and even quite into that of the critical appreciation of 'subject' in the novel". For, thanks to Turgenev, the "dull dispute" as to what is and is not "moral" had finally been resolved. The only question that really mattered was "is it genuine, is it sincere, the result of some direct impression or perception of life?" There was, he had realized (or at any rate realized when he came to write the Preface), a "perfect dependence of the 'moral' sense of a work of art on the amount of felt life concerned in producing it", so that the question really came back to the "kind and degree of the artist's prime sensibility".

These are the words of an artist who has "won through" to the true sources of his inspiration and to a confident enjoyment of them, and they are in marked contrast to the ceaseless debating and anxious self-examination of the earlier criticism. And he owed it in large measure to Turgenev that his ideas were no longer "tormented and disfigured and bemuddled". It was hardly surprising, therefore, that once he had begun to remember Turgenev's words, he should begin to remember also the great debt he owed him. "Other echoes from the same source linger with me, I confess, as unfadingly," he wrote—"if it be not all indeed one much-embracing echo."

It is *The Portrait of A Lady* that is the finest testimony of all to the potency of that "much embracing echo". It can indeed be heard in later novels, but seldom—to the ears, that is, of the reader—with such deep and far-ranging undertones. In *The Princess Casamassima*, for example, the influence is again rather at the obvious level of "resemblances"—to *Virgin Soil* in this instance. These were in fact so marked that they were easily detected by several of the contemporary periodicals. And James' comment on the character of Nezhdanov, that the main interest lies not merely in his faults and weaknesses but in his "exquisite consciousness" of his shortcomings, could be applied with equal justice to Hyacinth Robinson, who like Nezhdanov escapes from his *impasse* by suicide.

In many of the shorter pieces too, both those belonging to the period just before *The Portrait of A Lady* and those written later, the echo can be clearly heard. Catherine in *Washington Square*, for example (1880), reminds one of some of Turgenev's heroines, not only in her physical appearance but also in the conflict she suffers between the rival claims of passion and duty— which is, of course, the real purpose of the tale as it was of so many of Turgenev's (though the influence of Balzac's *Eugénie Grandet* is also apparent).

Again it is plausible to argue that Turgenev's *A Correspondence* had its effect, in subject matter and technique, both on James' *A Bundle of Letters* and on *The Point of View*, or that *The Dream* influenced *Master Eustace*, or even that Turgenev's tale of auto-suggestion *The Dog* contributed some effective touches to *The Turn of the Screw*.

In his later years, as he became increasingly self-confident, James modified many of his earlier ideas. His attitude towards morality, as the 1907 Preface shows, broadened. The violence of his antipathy towards the French Realists somewhat abated: his early admiration for Flaubert indeed underwent a considerable revival as he himself became increasingly preoccupied with problems of style. He tended perhaps in his later criticism to throw rather more stress on the Slav nature of Turgenev's genius. But at the same time he also laid greater emphasis (as in the article on Turgenev which he contributed to the 1902 edition of the *Library of the World's Best Literature*) upon the subjective quality of Turgenev's characters, on his portrayal of the world of the "inner consciousness"—and he may perhaps have encountered Turgenev's dictum that "the writer must be a psychologist, but a secret one: he must sense and know the roots of phenomena, but offer only the phenomena themselves—as they blossom or wither". And this indeed may be the significant point, suggesting not only that his estimate of Turgenev's genius kept pace with his own changing needs, but also that his influence had become part of his own creative blood-streams, taken in at a depth which left no surface coruscations, imperceptible to the mere critic, comprehensible only to the creator himself.

He had no doubt, for example, that it was Turgenev's inspiration that lay behind his own shorter pieces. In his *Notebooks*, under the date May 19th, 1889, he recorded a meeting with Taine who turned the conversation to Turgenev:

> ". . . his talk about him," James wrote, "has done me a world of good—reviving, refreshing, confirming, consecrating as it were the wish and dream that have lately grown stronger than ever in me—the desire that the literary heritage, such as it is, that I may leave, shall consist of a large number of perfect *short* things . . . and that they shall be fine, rare, strong, wise —eventually perhaps even recognized".

For Taine had reminded him of Turgenev's "depth, his variety, his form, the small perfect things he has left, which will live through their finished objectivity".

For James in fact the "much embracing echo" never faded. It was proof even against the realization that his own kind of Realism was not much to Turgenev's liking, "having on the surface too many little flowers and knots of ribbon", striking him as not "quite meat for men", as James ruefully puts it. The truth is that his gratitude was reinforced by a deep and lasting affection.

Turgenev's influence was a matter of the heart and the emotions as much as of the intellect. In every contact they had, he tells us, he found "something extraordinarily vivifying and stimulating": he never left him without being "in a state of intimate excitement, with a feeling that all sorts of valuable things had been suggested" to him. Turgenev was for him the ideal, both as man and artist, towards which James himself aspired.

"Ah, he was the real, but a thousand times the only—the only real beautiful genius!... One qualifies it with 'Russian' for immediateness of identification. But... for all of us who are ever so little in, as you might say, the know of literary values, he must be always just that, *tout court*—the beautiful genius."

CHAPTER SIX

THE NOVELISTS' NOVELIST

TURGENEV'S INFLUENCE ON SOME NOVELISTS OF THE NINETEENTH
CENTURY

"TURGENEV is in a peculiar degree what I may call the novelists'
novelist," Henry James wrote, "an artistic influence extraordinarily valuable, and ineradicably established."

It is not surprising therefore that in any examination of the
Russian influence Turgenev must occupy a preponderating part.
It is true that he began to recede into the background, both in
England and America, as first one and then another of his great
rivals loomed increasingly large, and eventually even his technique was called in question—Clutton Brock, for example,
accused him of being too narrow in his scope, too limited in
his effects, describing his novels as "exquisitely empty, like a
Japanese room".

But the fact remains—Turgenev has been "the novelists'
novelist" in a sense that cannot be applied to the other Russians,
and in consequence his reputation has always been safe in the
hands of those best qualified to preserve it—fellow practitioners
who care passionately for the craft of fiction. This does not mean,
however, that his admirers are to be found only among the more
deliberate craftsmen. Just as Spenser, "the poets' poet", exercises
a strange and sometimes fatal fascination over those who are
utterly different from him in temperament or natural gifts, so too
"the novelists' novelist" has attracted some surprising disciples.

GEORGE GISSING: 1875–1903

At first glance the suggestion that Turgenev was a powerful
influence in the work of George Gissing appears almost ludicrous :
his whole approach 'and method of composition, which strike
us today as so characteristically English, seem utterly recalcitrant
to it.

His interest in Russia itself is of course evident from his novels and particularly from *The Crown of Life* (1899), whose hero lives for many years in Russia and which has numerous references to Russian literature, politics and so on. We have Gissing's word for it too that the writers who were helping him most in his formative years were French and Russian, and his letters show that among these Russian writers Turgenev figured prominently. In 1883 for example he was writing to his sister Ellen, describing him as "without doubt the greatest living writer of fiction": a year later he was "very busy with Tourguénef", reading "five or six" of his novels in German. He was proud of the two letters which, he told Ellen, he had received from Turgenev "on matters of business"—probably in connection with a proposal that he should write a series of articles on English literature for the St. Petersburg periodical the *Messager de l'Europe*, and in another of the letters he proclaimed "he is a man I glory in".

It is generally assumed, however, that whatever Russian influence there is in Gissing derives from Dostoyevsky, and as we shall see there is some justification for this view. Nevertheless Turgenev was for him too, in his most impressionable period, "the novelists' novelist", and in some respects the influence of Dostoyevsky in his work has been exaggerated. Thus although his studies of "minds maddened by hunger" (as he expressed it in the book on Dickens) are Dostoyevskyan in their intensity, his approach is on the whole closer to Turgenev's. It is ethical and moral rather than psychological or mystical: even in the so-called "Dostoyevskyan" novels, such as *Workers in the Dawn* (1880), the main interest is concentrated on certain clear-cut moral problems which beset the characters, and as in Turgenev, the story is about the ways in which they resolve them. Character for both novelists is in fact the crux.

Gissing's portrayal of squalor and wretchedness, moreover, has no deep affinity with Dostoyevsky's. One of his main purposes, as he tells us himself, was to correct the over-optimistic picture presented by Dickens, and his Realism in this respect probably owes as much to Zola as it does to Dostoyevsky. He has had personal experience of poverty and suffering, and is in consequence able to communicate them faithfully, but his attitude towards them is often, particularly in the earlier books, one of resentment, open or concealed. He writes as a man who has been brought low by misfortune, but who feels himself fundamentally aloof from the environment into which it has forced him. The characters who engage his sympathy in his representations of slum life are those of "superior" status—artisans or members of the lower-middle classes, who also feel aloof from their surroundings. Of the masses as such he is bitterly scornful, and there is in fact a good deal of misanthropy in his earlier work. He reveals little of Dostoyevsky's emotional and imaginative identification with poverty, suffering and evil, and his pity and understanding in consequence are nothing like as profound.

His favourite characters in fact are closer to the types portrayed by Turgenev than to the curious, fluid, paradoxical, shifting figures of Dostoyevsky. The typical heroes—Golding in *Workers in the Dawn*, Egremont in *Thyrza* (1887), Weymark in *The Unclassed* (1884), to some extent Piers Otway in *The Crown of Life*, bear a clearly recognizable relationship to Dmitri Rudin or Nezhdanov. They have the same highly strung temperaments, and the same instability of purpose, particularly in relation to marriage, and all of them compare unfavourably with their womenfolk. They are usually possessed, moreover, of some high moral purpose. Sometimes this takes the form of an ideal which the hero has set before him, and sometimes he succeeds in attaining, or maintaining, it—Piers Otway, for example, eventually achieves his "crown of life" when he wins Irene's love. But often, as with Turgenev and James, the characters become "morally interesting" only in failure. Thus Annabel says to Egremont after Thyrza's death:

"The crisis of your life was there. There was your great opportunity, and you let it pass. She could not have lived; but that is no matter. You were tried, Mr. Egremont, and found wanting."

Egremont's betrayal of Thyrza, moreover, springs from the fundamental falsity of his position in relation to "the people" in a way that vividly recalls Dmitri Rudin and Nezhdanov. Like them he is young, cultured, of superior birth and breeding, full of vague aspirations and yearnings, and vexed by a social conscience. Like them he is in revolt against the privileges and conventions of his class, and endeavours to find an outlet for his personal insecurities and dissatisfactions by "going to the people". Like them he remains, in spite of his sensitivity and the sincerity of his desire to serve, irrevocably of his own class, and his essential remoteness is thrown into relief by his association with genuine men of the people—thus Nezhdanov's relationship with Solomin is echoed by that of Egremont with Gilbert Grail, and in the event Egremont like Nezhdanov, though his solution is neither as drastic nor as heroic, runs away from his *impasse*.

There are of course vast differences in the environments and conditions against which the two novelists operate, but Egremont illustrates much the same sort of response to social change and the challenges that accompany it as do Rudin and Nezhdanov. Fundamentally there is here no difference between the Revolutionary and the Adult Education Lecturer.

This patterning in Gissing admittedly does not derive from Turgenev's influence alone. To some extent it is yet another instance of a certain similarity in social environments producing a certain similarity in fictional types. For Gissing too, as Morley Roberts pointed out in his Preface to the 1927 edition of *Thyrza*, was, like so many of his characters, a "man of exile"; he was the product of a society in a state of flux, a man who felt himself without a real class of his own, or a real place in the social structure into which he was born. This is also of course a characteristic artist's predicament, one that besets many artists in many periods of civilization. In a sense the artist is always an exile, and this is perhaps one of the most important reasons why Turgenev, with his portraits of alienation which are almost universal prototypes, has become "the novelists' novelist".

Nevertheless it seems clear that in the writing of many of his novels Gissing was following Turgenev's example in a more straightforward sense. Egremont in *Thyrza* is not merely the repetition of a basic type, and indeed a specific hint that Gissing was thinking of Turgenev as he wrote is provided by Mr. Newthorpe's statement that he feels he is just the kind of character of whom Turgenev would have made "an admirable study". In *Isabel Clarendon* (1886) there are clues of a similar nature. For example, Thomas Meres urges Ada to read a novel by Turgenev in which he is confident she will "rejoice". This was probably *Fathers and Children*, and indeed there are recognizable echoes of Turgenev's novel to be found in Gissing's. Isabel's situation, for example, is similar to that of Anna Sergyevna ("how clearly I see Mme Odintsoff!" Gissing wrote to Ellen): she is not of course so much the *femme fatale*, she is warmer, and very English, with a good deal in common with some of Trollope's heroines, but in her weakness for society and for creature comforts even at the expense of integrity and of genuine passion, she reminds one of Bazarov's temptress, while her relationship to Ada recalls that of Anna Sergyevna to Katya. It is however in the portrayal of his curious, and not particularly likeable hero Kingcote, that the Russian influence is particularly apparent. It was of Kingcote, presumably, that Morley Roberts was thinking when, in his Preface to *Thyrza*, he wrote of *Isabel Clarendon* as above all revealing "its Russian affinities and his own temperament, equally plainly akin to many of the Russian writers from Turgenev onward".

Now we know from Gissing's letters that Bazarov made a powerful impression on him—"a wonderfully drawn character" he told Ellen when at last he had persuaded her to read *Fathers and Children*. And his description of him in the same letter as an example of "the purely negative mind, common enough nowadays in men of thought" is certainly applicable to Kingcote. More appropriately indeed than to Bazarov himself who, after all, as a person is by no means "purely negative", and whose Nihilism, unsatisfactory though it may be as a progressive doctrine of action, does not preclude hard work, and a belief both in Science and in himself. Kingcote is typical rather of the Western interpretation of the word "Nihilism" (Gissing incidentally uses it in his letter to Ellen) and in his case it involves an almost complete abnegation of effort.

He is closer to Bazarov, however, in some of his nihilistic utterances, particularly in those calculated to "shock the bourgeoisie". He surprises Mrs. Stratton, for example, by agreeing with her, though with a passion she had hardly bargained for, about the exaggerated importance attached to Education, and in much the same way he pours scorn on all the other accepted traditions and conventions of society. Like Bazarov too he has no use for the "sentimental" beliefs of Liberalism and he is as scathing as he is about the peasantry.

> "At times I talk with a farm labourer . . . to do so I have to divest myself of the last rag of civilization, to strip my mind to its kernel. Were oxen suddenly endowed with speech they would utter themselves as these peasants do. . . ."

Kingcote has little of Bazarov's inherent strength of character, and his negativism is personal and psychological rather than doctrinaire—Bazarov, for example, would have scorned Kingcote's misanthropy as itself a sentimental indulgence. At bottom in fact he is a Liberal idealist (of the type that Gissing was to portray a year later in Egremont) who has become so disillusioned that he speaks with the negativism of Bazarov, but with a personal bitterness that Bazarov does not possess. It is as if Arkady and Bazarov had somehow become merged into one and the mixture had turned sour.

Even for Gissing, moreover, unlikely though it may seem, Turgenev was "the novelists' novelist" in a more narrowly technical sense. When in a letter of 1885 for example he criticizes the old-fashioned English three-decker novel, and states his belief in "the later method of merely suggesting, of dealing with episodes, instead of writing biographies" as "far more artistic", it is obvious that he is thinking of Turgenev, six of whose novels, as we have seen, he had bought in German translation the year before. He sounds, indeed, almost as if he had joined the Atlantic Monthly school when he goes on to deplore the old "omniscient" novelist.

> "I think it is better," he writes, "to tell a story precisely as one does in real life, hinting, surmising, telling in detail what can be told, and no more. In fact, it approximates to the dramatic mode of presentment."

These are curious pronouncements coming from Gissing, whose novels seem so thoroughly English in their leisurely narration and looseness of structure—and indeed it was only a year later that *Isabel Clarendon* was published in three volumes. The novel is certainly the reverse of Turgenev's delicately moulded structures, but there is no doubt that Gissing, like so many other English novelists who themselves conspicuously lacked the Russian's qualities of grace and economy, set him up as his ideal. There are indeed signs in *Isabel Clarendon* of an attempt to put the precepts he had formulated in his letter into practice : much of the "character analysis" of the hero, for example, which Gissing, in the traditional English way, would have normally conducted himself, is "dramatically" communicated by Kingcote —often, it must be admitted, in long and clumsy speeches which merely sound like author's comment put in inverted commas.

It was, in fact, those who were by nature better suited to the ideal of Form in fiction who found Turgenev's influence most valuable. For them indeed he *was* the Russian Novel, and there was no question of his great contemporaries ever replacing him. Thus Henry James, although he admitted that Tolstoy represented "a wonderful mass of life", and that the reading of one of his novels must be regarded as "an immense event", pointed out that he could exercise "no such external spell of method, no such quiet irresistibility of presentation" as shines from the pages of Turgenev "lighting our possible steps". Tolstoy in fact appeared to him as "a reflector, as vast as a natural lake ; a monster harnessed, for purposes of traction, not to a carriage but to a coach house". His own case was indeed "prodigious", but as an example for others it was "dire", and "disciples not elephantine" he could but "mislead and betray".

Indeed it seemed to James that Tolstoy *had* misled and betrayed, diverting the Novel from its true path and function. In discussing a group of Georgian novelists in 1914 he deplored the absence of any genuine centre of interest, the lack of composition, structure, fusion—qualities that all belonged abundantly to Turgenev—and ascribed these deficiencies to the influence of Tolstoy, "the great illustrative master hand in all this ground of the disconnection of method from matter". And if Tolstoy seemed formless to James and those who thought like him it can be imagined that the "Russian fever" centred upon Dostoyevsky must have seemed so much sound and fury.

For James and his school indeed both Tolstoy and Dostoyev-sky were "fluid puddings"—not tasteless, James conceded, as in the case of their misguided followers, because their great qualities of mind and soul and "the strong, rank quality of their genius" brought "flavour and favour"—but "fluid puddings" neverthe-less. For it was "Form alone," James declared, "that takes and holds and preserves substance, and saves it from the welter of helpless verbiage."

And to all those who believed as James believed, Turgenev was a model of classical grace and proportion, the natural and inevitable "novelists' novelist". From the very beginning indeed, as we have seen, and even at a stage when interest tended to be focussed on the political aspects of his work, he was hailed as the supreme example of the "artist" in fiction. There were small élites long before what Arnold Bennett described as "the great Turgenev vogue" began. In the 1870s, for example, he was a subject of ardent discussion among Ann Sidgwick and her circle and in 1880 *Blackwood's Edinburgh Magazine* was speaking of "a Turgenev cult" among "the leading intelligences".

But it was in the 1890s among the supporters of the Aesthetic Movement (and just at the time, incidentally, when critics such as Baring and Brückner were launching their attacks) that Tur-genev naturally found some of his most devoted adherents. Thus Oscar Wilde, much as he deplored Realism as a method, because it did not put Beauty as its main objective, approved of the "imaginative realism" of the Russians, of whom, he wrote in the *Pall Mall Gazette*, Turgenev was "by far the finest artist". Turgenev, in association with Flaubert, was also the idol of the "Henley Gang". The centre of the cult perhaps was to be found in the group of writers gathered round Ford Madox Ford, "the Conrad-James-Crane school" as he once called it. To this band of devotees indeed Turgenev appeared not only as that "fabulous monster, a natural genius", but also as a profound moral influence.

"I am sure," Ford wrote in later life, echoing the similar profession of Henry James, "that if ever I—and how many others!—committed ourselves to little good and kindly actions or courses of life, it was because we in our youths fell under the influence of that beautiful and lambent spirit. . . ."

And the Turgenev cult may be said to have reached its climax when Ford proclaimed "We are pretty certain that Turgenev was greater than Shakespeare. . . . His characters are more human than Shakespeare's were," and Frank Harris declared that Shakespeare could not have created a Bazarov or a Marianna.

GEORGE MOORE: 1852–1933

Perhaps the most considerable and instructive example of his influence on the disciples of Form on this side of the Atlantic, however, is to be found in the work of George Moore. It is true that when one recalls the ease with which Moore took up and abandoned first one and then another enthusiasm one tends to be sceptical of his ability to react anything but superficially to any influence. But in fact Turgenev's influence was one of his really profound aesthetic experiences, which more perhaps than any other had the effect, at a crucial point in his career, of turning him inwards to find his own kind of originality, to touch the springs of his own creativity.

The discovery of Turgenev indeed marked the climax of his formative phase in much the same way that it did for Henry James, and their early pilgrimages, culminating in a deep personal understanding of Turgenev's aims and methods, follow roughly similar lines of development. Like James, Moore began his career as a determined and deliberate disciple of the French Realists, though in his case the attraction was more specifically for Naturalism itself. As a young man he assiduously cultivated Zola's acquaintance. He took care, for example, to send him the article which he wrote in 1882, proudly informing him that it was "the first eulogy" he had received in England. His early novels were obviously written under Zola's influence. *A Modern Lover* (1883) achieved the distinction of being banned by the Circulating Libraries, and when in spite of this it attracted considerable attention Moore wrote to Zola ". . . the fact that my novel has been successful may interest you; for as I have already told you, I owe you everything." Both *A Mummer's Wife* (1884) and *A Drama in Muslin* (1886) reveal the typical Naturalistic techniques —the careful descriptions of background, based on careful research, the emphasis on environmental factors, the deliberately unidealized characterization, and of course the unsavoury elements which earned from some of the reviewers the kind of response usually reserved for Zola himself—the *Academy*, for example, declared of *A Drama in Muslin* that "a more repulsive" tale had never been written. *Parnell and his Island* (1887) also exhibits the familiar signs of Zola's influence, especially in the chapter on the Irish peasants. And when Vizetelly published *Piping Hot* it was George Moore, by natural prerogative, who wrote the Preface, in which he dutifully praised the Master as "one of the mighty monumental intelligences of all time", and as "the Homer of modern life".

But *Parnell and his Island* was the last of Moore's books to adopt a whole-hearted Naturalistic technique, though vestiges of it remain in some of the later books, including *Esther Waters* (1894). As in James' case, moreover, and in spite of his ardent assumption of the rôle of the English Zola, there were all along signs that he too was not really exempt from the typical English yearning after romantic and idealist sanctions. He responded eagerly, for example, to Pater's *Marius the Epicurean*. Huysman's *A Rebours* filled him with enthusiasm, and his own novel *A Mere Accident* (1887) was probably inspired by it.

His allegiance to Zola continued, however, until 1888, when the famous visit to Médan which marked the beginning of the final break took place. It was a meeting which reminds one in many respects of Henry James' journey to Paris in 1875. In both cases the result was a disillusionment which marked the climax of the years of apprenticeship. In later life Moore suggested that he should really be considered as two writers—the real George Moore, and a younger disciple, Amico Moorini, the raw young man portrayed in *The Confessions* (1888). It was Amico Moorini, one feels, who went to visit Zola at Médan; it was George Moore who returned.

The main agent in the transition, as in the case of Henry James, was Turgenev, whom he met in this same year. And the

G

article which he wrote about him for the *Fortnightly Review* some months later reveals the extent to which Turgenev has helped him towards a reassessment of his own aims as a writer.

In the light of his example, it now seems to him, the doctrines of Naturalism are exposed as false, materialistic and self-contradictory. It is clear to him that the "indifferent" objectivity of their methods is a myth, and an ugly one at that: Flaubert's much vaunted "impersonality", for example, suddenly appears to him empty and arid. Far more fruitful is Turgenev's "subjective" approach, whereby even the description of external phenomena is suffused by the glow of his personality and spirit.

To Moore, in consequence, the question seemed now not so much a matter of opposition between Realist and Romantic, Idealist or Naturalist, but one between "fact mind" and "thought mind". Thus Zola's strength lay in "fact mind", and Turgenev's in "thought mind".

> "What I wish to establish," he wrote, "is that it is a vain and fruitless task to narrate any fact unless it has been tempered and purified in thought, and stamped by thought with specific value."

As in the case of James, the importance of Turgenev's influence in the first instance lies not so much in actual attempts to imitate his methods as in the part it played in stimulating and nourishing his own genius, in confirming and strengthening predilections hitherto unrecognized, and in precipitating him from the youthful experimentations of Amico Moorini into the maturity of George Moore. It was not of course a sudden process. At this stage he is still showing a hankering after the excitements of Zola, the scope, the noise, and the bustle. Other continental influences were also important in drawing him away from Zola. There was Huysmans as we have seen, and there was also Gautier and the Symbolists, though very shortly these were to seem "like walnuts and wine", merely "an agreeable after taste" and to be supplanted by Flaubert, in spite of the strictures of the Turgenev essay. The Flaubert of Style and Form, that is, not Flaubert the Naturalist—and it is his influence more than any other that lies behind *Esther Waters* (1894). Balzac and Maupassant were also important influences and ones which remained with him all his life. By comparison with some of these writers indeed Turgenev, in 1888, seemed to him to lack variety and boldness, to be too "reserved". And although he did not, like Flaubert, try to force his Art down our throats "with a steel fork", he was perhaps *too* conscious an artist. He appeared to Moore at this point in fact as a "beautifully cultivated islet, lying somewhere between the philosophic realism of Balzac and the maiden-lady realism of Miss Austen".

But gradually, as in the case of James, his appreciation of Turgenev changed and deepened as he himself changed and deepened, so that it ran parallel with and interpenetrated all the later currents that entered into his work, eventually perhaps superseding them all. It kept pace, for example, with his growing sympathy with the Aesthetic Movement, foreshadowed by his earlier admiration of Pater, and it flowed side by side with the influences of French Impressionism and the Celtic Revival. In his later criticism there is no sign of the reservations of the 1888 article. Turgenev's stories appear now "as shapely as Greek vases . . . the most comely stories in the world". Turgenev becomes for him, as for James, the perfect artist, disciplined in his craft, disdainful of mere cleverness, concerned always with balance and proportion. And at the same time he is deep and subtle and humane: although, for example (according to Moore), he is fundamentally indifferent to political causes, he reacts instinctively to human suffering and has not the slightest touch of the moral insensitivity which mars the work of Flaubert and Maupassant.

As his admiration of Turgenev steadily increased, moreover, he found himself, like James, incapable of fully appreciating any of the other Russian novelists. He had shown some interest in Dostoyevsky, writing the Preface to Lena Milman's translations of *Poor Folk* in 1884, and at one point he had proclaimed *Anna Karenina* "the greatest novel ever written". But neither Dostoyevsky nor Tolstoy could in his estimate hold a candle to Turgenev. Put Turgenev beside Tolstoy and he seemed "neither cab nor dray" (perhaps he had James' image of the coach-house in mind) "but an Arab carrying in every story a lady as romantic as one of Chopin's ballads", while Dostoyevsky was "Gaboriau with psychological sauce, and that of an inferior kind". In Turgenev there was none of the "tumult and vapour" that obscured the pages of Tolstoy and Dostoyevsky. Even in content and moral force Turgenev was superior, for he was not satisfied with the mere surface of life; he saw the "shadowy subterranean design" —unlike Tolstoy who was lord only "over what is actual and passing", and who "built a palatial hotel" which contained everything but beauty and poetry.

Turgenev in fact became more and more the real touchstone of his literary, moral, and aesthetic values. In the sphere of practical influence his presence can be felt as early as 1889 in *Mike Fletcher* (though it is one of the books which Moore suggested should be ascribed to Amico Moorini), where the hero's long cogitation culminating in suicide is strongly suggestive of Nezhdanov in *Virgin Soil*.

More interesting, however, is the case of *Evelyn Innes* (1896). It is true that in his later years he came to the conclusion that this book was not fit even for Amico Moorini, and hoped that posterity could exclude it from the "canon" altogether. As a novel indeed it never convinces, in spite of its fascination as a repository of Moore's impressions and opinions, on French fiction, painting, food, and manners, on women's dress and women's beauty, on mediaeval music, on Celtic mythology, and a dozen other topics.

Nevertheless Moore did feel that *Evelyn Innes* was at least an example of "thought mind" as opposed to "fact mind", and at the outset he was far from modest about it. "It is," he wrote to his brother, "inferior to Tourgournoff" (surely the most curious transliteration of all) "and Balzac, but I think it is better than trashy Thackeray, and rubbishy Dickens, and pompous Eliot," and his modesty in relation to Turgenev does in fact point to various attempts in the course of the book to benefit from his influence.

It is apparent, for example, in the tone and atmosphere of some of the descriptions of natural scenery. Thus when Evelyn is walking with Owen near his home after his mother's death,

"she wondered at the strange somnolent life of the cattle in the meadows and the swans on the pond . . . the stillness of the summer was in every blade of grass, in every leaf, and the pond reflected the sky and willows, in hard, immovable reflections. An occasional ripple of the water-fowl in the reeds impressed upon them the mystery of Nature's indifference to human suffering."

In many ways it is a curiously static piece of Nature description, and in fact the details, as in many of Turgenev's landscapes, are completely subservient to the human protagonists and their situation. And it is illuminating in this context to recall a remark made by Steer the painter, to the effect that when Moore described a scene it seemed to be based upon a *picture* rather than upon direct observation—and when he was writing *The Brook Kerith* (1916) we know that it was a sketch by Tonks which inspired the scene in which Joseph and his tutor play truant in the countryside round Arimathea. Turgenev, too, expressed surprise when one of his visitors commented on his "landscapes"—and assured him that it was character alone that he took seriously. Similarly, when Holt the American publisher commented on the view from Turgenev's window at Bougival he replied with some impatience "this means nothing to me". In fact neither Turgenev nor Moore regarded himself as primarily a Nature writer, and Moore, like Turgenev, "composed" his landscapes primarily in order to communicate the mood and feelings of his characters.

In some other respects too *Evelyn Innes* recalls Turgenev. In his 1888 article Moore had singled out for special praise Turgenev's power of fusing physical details and mental impressions, and he quotes in particular the scene in *Fathers and Children* where Anna Sergyevna questions herself about Bazarov, as she lies under her silk coverlet—a scene which, Moore observes, makes the reader conscious at one and the same time of her actual physical presence, and of the internal reverie. In *Evelyn Innes* there are so many occasions on which one is introduced to the heroine communing with herself as she dresses, brushes her hair, drives in her carriage, rests on her couch, or eats her lunch that the device becomes monotonous, and it is clear that Moore is deliberately testing out the new technique.

Some of the touches of character portraiture, too, have a sharpness of focus, a satirical edge, which are strongly reminiscent of Turgenev. The description of Sir Owen, for example, with his pale brown hair "curling a little at the ends, and carefully brushed and looking as if it had been freshened by some faintest application of perfumed essence", somehow seems more appropriate to one of Turgenev's minor characters, for example, Panshin in *A Nest of Gentlefolk*. It is probably no accident, moreover, that *Evelyn Innes* is a novel which turns on a problem of conscience, and that the heroine, like Lisa in *A Nest of Gentlefolk*, seeks refuge from her difficulties by entering a convent—though in the later version of his novel Moore decided that Evelyn's vocation was not, after all, for the life of a nun, and he turned her—latterday apotheosis—into a Social Worker instead. Finally this novel is perhaps the first to show Moore fully aware of his desire to escape from the Naturalistic formulae, and to introduce idealism, romance, and sensibility into his work—and there are indeed long passages in it which are rather tracts designed to expound these issues than genuine fiction. In his 1888 article, however, Moore seizes with particular enthusiasm upon Turgenev's shorter works. In this field he finds the Russian "standing quite alone, towering above all competitors". What, he demands, has England or France to put beside *A Sportsman's Sketches*? One would have to turn to the *Arabian Nights*, he suggests, to find anything at all comparable to the curious abruptness and freedom from conventional psychology that they display.

It seems to him that by these means Turgenev is able to lay bare "not the body, but rather the nerve" of an emotion or a passion, and to indicate that which is "most individual and constitutional" in a character. He marvels at his subtlety, economy, and delicacy of touch: "He would show you a face," Moore observes, "and he would not stop to impress you by the exaggeration of a single feature; a little, a very little human passion seen carefully, seen at a curious, but not too curious, angle will do." Yet in spite of this restraint the narrative "rushes forth", proceeding without the slightest hesitation or stop, so that the reader has no idea what is going to happen next, although at the same time the incidents are chosen with such care that they follow each other "without jostling or discord", so that when they come into the reader's mind he is surprised at once by their "naturalness and unexpectedness". And what above all fascinates Moore is that this method, in spite of the absence of detail and elaborate analysis of motive, is a genuinely *realistic* one, that the illusion produced "is of life itself", and that "a mere narrative, I will say a bare narrative" can possess as much "intellectual charm" as a whole psychological novel by Flaubert.

Although in his latest phase Moore liked to boast of the ancient classical and oriental affinities in his narrative manner, and though there are touches which suggest Maupassant, there is no doubt that Turgenev was the major influence behind his shorter pieces, and indeed in the choice of the form itself. It began to make itself felt in his short stories soon after the 1888 article, particularly in the tales which later appeared in *Celibates* (1895—the title was changed to *In Single Strictness* and *Celibate Lives* in other editions). Some of these early tales seemed to him to be utter failures—*Hugh Monfert*, for example, he described as "a damp squib"—but of some of the others he was very proud, and for the very reason that he believed they successfully incorporated the principles which Turgenev exemplified. Thus when John Eglinton ventured to criticize some of them Moore retorted :

> "It may be you have not been at pains to compare these stories with other psychological stories. There are not many psychological stories in the English language, but Tourguenieff has been translated, and I ask you to say, hand on heart, that you thought of *Sarah Gwynn* in connection with Tourguenieff, and came to the conclusion that Tourguenieff would not have done more with the subject than I did."

It is difficult perhaps not to agree with Eglinton's scepticism, and it is certainly difficult, hand on heart, to compare *Sarah Gwynn* with anything in Turgenev. It is clear, though, that he is after the same kind of effect : he too has tried to construct "an entire personality" by means of delicate shading and stippling, without reliance upon accumulation of detail or elaborate psychological analysis.

He is more successful in these aims and also closer to Turgenev in *Wilfrid Holmes*, which was one of his own favourites. Wilfrid is a futile, dreary character of the type that might well be found on the fringes of a Turgenev novel. His futility, more-over, is of a special kind, deriving not only from his own innate incapacity, but also from the fact that he is the representative of a phase of nineteenth-century social history—a man left over from a vanishing social order which alone could have provided a haven for his mediocrity. Moore is of course observing a real situation, and he was not the only English novelist of the period to make use of it. There is little doubt, however, that Moore, like Gissing, has in mind Turgenev's prototypes of disorientation when he wrote the story—and one suspects that it is *The Diary of A Superfluous Man* which is the specific influence. In the method of narration Turgenev's influence is obvious, and Moore relates poor Wilfrid's ineffectual efforts as musician, scholar, and writer with something of his blend of irony and pity.

But none of these stories—neither *Sarah Gwynn* nor *Wilfrid Holmes* nor *Henrietta Marr*, which come closest perhaps to Turgenev in tone and narrative shape, nor *Agnes Lahens* which has also been likened to Turgenev—ever really generates imaginative heat or fuses into a significant whole. Moore does indeed achieve something of the "unexpectedness" which he had noted in Turgenev's tales, but without their freshness and narrative pres-sure. Instead of achieving "the melodic line" which he so much admired in Turgenev (and which from now on was to be his almost continuous preoccupation) he achieves merely an air of inconsequentiality.

It is a different matter, however, with *The Untilled Field* (1903). Here again the major influence, in tone, method, and subject-matter, is that of Turgenev—an influence which is of course in this case well authenticated and acknowledged by Moore himself. The genesis of the book, he tells us in his Preface to *The Lake* (1905), lay in "some chance words" which he had with John Eglinton, as they returned home one evening from Professor Dowden's—"He spoke, or I spoke, of a volume of Irish stories" and "Tourguéniev's name was mentioned" . . . His first reaction, according to Eglinton's account, was to exclaim "As well ask me to paint like Corot." Nevertheless he determined to accept his friend's challenge to become "the Irish Turgenev".

The tales that resulted were, unlike so many of the earlier ones, something more than technical exercises in the Turgenev manner. Behind them lay a genuine imaginative and emotional pressure, provided by his return to Ireland and his *rapprochement* with the Celtic Movement. Real feeling combined with technical influence to produce some of his most successful work, and Moore brings to these simple studies of Irish peasant life something of the freshness, naturalness and tenderness that we find in *A Sportsman's Sketches*.

The superficial resemblances are obvious. There are the same transcripts of peasant life, the same basic situations which illustrate peasant simplicity, or cunning, related with a gentle humour and irony. In the background in both cases lie the masters, lords of the manor or parish priests, usually aloof and mysterious forces with strange whims which have to be reckoned with on the same basis as health or the weather.

Turgenev's influence is evident too in the tone and atmosphere of the tales—in the use of sky, cloud, and water to convey mood and character. Above all it is apparent in the technique—the freedom from conventional dramatic shaping, the lack of an obvious climax, and the gentle dying fall, leaving an effect not of inconclusiveness (as in so many of Moore's earlier tales) but of a conclusion infinitely deferred or fading slowly away like wisps of cloud in a sunset sky. Some of the tales in *The Untilled Field* it is true are flat and thin compared with Turgenev's: they lack his power of concentrating within a tiny area an extraordinarily potent charge of poetic emotion. If anything, too, the search after Turgenev's simplicity and spontaneity is too deliberate, and sometimes contrived. In actual fact Turgenev allows himself to comment in his tales more than some of those who praised him for his "dramatic" self-exclusion would allow, and here Moore practises a forbearance which is sometimes chilling. It is as if he is so anxious to keep his eye on "the melodic line" that he fails to give his themes proper breathing space, so that often their essence is not released at all.

But many of these defects have disappeared in *The Lake* (1905), the short novel which, as Moore explains in the Preface, really belongs to *The Untilled Field*, the outcome of

"the same happy inspiration . . . the return of a man to his native land, to its people, to memories hidden for years, forgotten, but which rose suddenly out of the darkness like water out of the earth when a spring is tapped".

Here in spite of occasional preciosity the emotion is stronger than the aesthetic preoccupation, and *The Lake* is perhaps the most fruitful instance of Turgenev's influence, as it is perhaps Moore's most subtle and moving book.

It is easy to discover, with more or less plausibility, superficial resemblances between *The Lake* and Turgenev's work. But the real importance of Turgenev's influence in *The Lake* lies at a deeper level. It can be seen for example in the way in which Moore's memories of boyhood, his reflections on Irish history and traditions, his snatches of peasant gossip and folklore are all presented through Father Oliver's reveries in a way that recalls Turgenev's musings on similar themes in *A Sportsman's Sketches* (in his case, too, usually based on boyhood memories and thus to some extent re-creations of "emotion recollected in tranquility"). These reflections, moreover, take place in both instances against a background of sky, woodland and water. . . . But here "background" is the wrong word, just as it is for Turgenev. The tenderly lyrical descriptions of lake, clouds, the pearl and rose-coloured sky, and the sudden foreshortenings of perspective to take in minutely observed details—reeds, birds, insects—all pass through Father Oliver's consciousness as they do through that of the "rapt watcher" in *A Sportsman's Sketches* or through the minds of so many of Turgenev's heroes and heroines—all producing a total effect not primarily of landscape at all but of *character*. The scenes in which they move are not separate and external, they are parts of their own consciousness or extensions of it, surrounding them like a nimbus. We can see this interweaving of thought, act, mood, atmosphere, observation, and scene at the very beginning of *The Lake*:

"It was one of those enticing days at the beginning of May when white clouds are drawn about the earth like curtains. The lake lay like a mirror that somebody had breathed upon. The brown islands showing through the mist faintly, with grey shadows falling into the water, blurred at the edges. The ducks were talking in the reeds, and the reeds themselves were talking, and the water lapping softly about the smooth limestone shingle. But there was an impulse in the gentle day, and turning from the sandy spit, Father Oliver walked to and fro along the disused cart-track about the edge of the wood, asking himself if he was going home, knowing very well that he could not bring himself to interview his parishioners that morning. . . ."

In a passage such as this how can one tell where the evocation of scene ends and that of the human situation begins? Father Oliver, for example, is at the beginning of a new Spring, though self-torturing doubts are "like curtains" that hide the realization from him. Like "the brown islands" in the distance his own future is uncertain and his own conception of it "blurred at the edges". The ducks and the reeds and the water talk incessantly, in unison with his own ceaseless self-questionings. The "disused cart-track" once had its destination, but is now purposeless: there is an "impulse in the gentle day" which draws him away from the duties which were once his clearly defined goal. And above all, always present in Father Oliver's consciousness, there is the Lake—or is it a mirror, misty at the moment as if some-body had breathed upon it, in which he will one day see his destiny?

And at the end of the story the symbolism of the lake takes on a final subtlety and depth. Father Oliver has swum across the lake, leaving his priest's clothes and his priest's identity behind him: he has put on the clothes he had previously hidden on the farther shore and is sitting in the train that will take him to Cork and thence to his New World:

"'I shall never see that lake again, but I shall never forget it,' and as he dozed in a corner of an empty carriage, the spectral light of the lake awoke him, and when he arrived at Cork it seemed to him that he was being engulfed in the deep pool by the Joycetown shore. On the deck of the steamer he heard the lake's warble above the violence of the waves. 'There is a lake in every man's heart,' he said, 'and he listens to its monotonous whisper year by year, more and more attentive till at last he ungirds.'"

Here the fusion of natural object and human emotion—in spite of the perversely "clever" final word—is as effective as anything Moore wrote. In his later work, as in James', the influence of Turgenev is not as close to the surface as in the examples we have noted—though there are passages in *Memoirs of My Dead Life* (1928) in which it is again clearly recognizable, and the tone of much of Moore's self-revelation recalls that of Turgenev in the *Prose Poems*. On the whole, however, it was overlaid by later influences, particularly that of the Celtic Revival and his growing preoccupation with Theology. In many respects his later development seems to take him away from the mainstream of modern fiction. He set out deliberately to widen the gap between himself and the English tradition. He was farther removed from it than either George Gissing or Henry James. He was harsher in his strictures on English fiction than either of them. He was exasperated by the English novelist's habit of intruding himself into his story, and he deplored the lack of discipline and unity which he found in the majority of English novels; unlike Gissing and James, he failed to understand that there were virtues to compensate for their shapelessness. His reaction against the French Realists too was more extreme than theirs. He was convinced that, with Turgenev's help, he was aiming at an art more subtle than that of the Realistic novel, that his "melodic line" was far superior to the plot-construction of the contemporary novel, French or English, that through it he was reviving the lost tradition of storytelling and producing work more in tune with the ancient storytellers, classical, oriental, mediaeval, and Celtic. He pushed his theories to an extreme in some of his later novels, so that when the first enthusiasm that greeted them had died away they seemed to be pallid and self-conscious exercises in Applied Art, completely divorced from the living European tradition.

As far as Turgenev was concerned too he tended to exaggerate the classicism of his art and to forget that Turgenev in fact allowed himself a good deal of personal comment and exposition, and that he was also the heir of Pushkin and Gogol, with a strong admixture of old-fashioned Byronic romanticism and passion to agitate the "classical contours". In some respects indeed Moore and his followers did Turgenev's reputation a disservice by diverting it into the cause of a somewhat narrow concept of Art just at the time when Tolstoy and Dostoyevsky were beginning to gain the ascendancy.

Whatever the final assessment of George Moore may be, however, there can be no doubt of his gratitude to Turgenev. Like James he never forgot his meetings with him in Paris, the spell which the "amiable giant" cast upon him both as a man and as a writer, or the debt he owed him. He knew that he would never have achieved as much or as well as he did without the inspiration of his example, and that "the translucence of Turgenev" (to use the phrase which Charles Morgan has applied to Moore) shines through his best work. Turgenev and Corot remained the major influences of his life—"They have been and still are," he wrote as an old man, "the holy places where I rested and rest; together they have revealed to me all that I need to know."

CHAPTER SEVEN

THE NOVELISTS' NOVELIST AND
MRS. BROWN

TURGENEV'S INFLUENCE ON SOME ENGLISH NOVELISTS OF THE TWENTIETH CENTURY

WHEN in the 1920s Virginia Woolf came to examine the condition of the contemporary novel, it seemed to her that writers such as Arnold Bennett, John Galsworthy and H. G. Wells were fundamentally materialists, concerned "not with the spirit, but with the body", writers who spent "immense skill and immense industry making the trivial and the transitory appear the true and the enduring". They were the kind of novelists, she declared in her lecture on "Mr. Bennett and Mrs. Brown",[1] who if they had met her imaginary old lady Mrs. Brown in a railway carriage, would have wanted merely to count the buttons, the ribbons, the wrinkles and the warts.

Virginia Woolf was hardly just, however, in ascribing to these writers exclusively materialistic preoccupations. All of them believed that they were in fact revealing the deeper truths behind external phenomena, and all of them had hankerings after a more poetic, evocative approach.

ARNOLD BENNETT: 1867–1931

These yearnings can often be seen in relation to Turgenev. This is true even of Arnold Bennett who seemed to Virginia Woolf the most materialistic of all the Georgians. The major influence in his work, it is true, was that of the French Realists, and on the whole it was an enduring one. But he too experienced a moment at which their methods seemed inadequate, leaving him with the uneasy feeling that something in life had escaped him. As with most of his contemporaries it was in the Russian

[1] Given to the Heretics, Cambridge, May 18th, 1924.

Novel that he found the compromise he was seeking, and in the 1890s that in the main still meant Turgenev. After reading *Virgin Soil*, for example, he decides, as he tells us in his *Journals* (1932–3), that Turgenev is without doubt the "greatest master of the modern novel". He ruefully comes to the conclusion that he himself knows "practically nothing" about "development of character", making up his mind that in future he will follow Turgenev's practice of sketching the previous history and background of each of his characters. Just over a year later (January 11th, 1898) we see him deciding, with Mr. Eden Phillpotts' approval, that he must "deal thoroughly" with Turgenev. By 1899 he is proclaiming that the period of his enthusiasm for French Naturalism is over, and a year later he is admitting in an article in the *Academy* that in the past he had "attached too high a value to realism". His aim now, he declares, is to "depict the deeper beauty while abiding by the envelope of facts".

And although Tolstoy and later Dostoyevsky and Chekhov challenged Turgenev for the first place in his favour, in matters of pure technique Turgenev remained the model. *On the Eve*, long after he had ostensibly transferred his allegiance to the other Russians, seemed to him "the most perfect example of the novel yet produced in any country". Turgenev may have lacked the fiery vehemence of Tolstoy, but as an *artist* he had "hardly a fault". Dostoyevsky may have been greater, but he could never have achieved the technical perfection, the "calm and exquisite soft beauty" of *On the Eve* and *A Nest of Gentlefolk*. And as late as 1924 we find him once again citing Turgenev as the only novelist who really knew what fictional technique meant—proudly adding "I thank heaven I have always gone in for technique. And *The Pretty Lady* and *Riceyman Steps* are both in my opinion jolly well constructed and *done* books."

However doggedly Bennett may have "gone in for technique", however, one is hard put to it to find anything in either of the two novels he mentions, or in any of the others, that bears real comparison with Turgenev. One can detect the attempts to approximate to the Turgenev atmosphere perhaps in some of the love scenes and their relation to natural backgrounds : the youthful Sophia in *The Old Wives' Tale* (1908) has a suggestion of the wilful charm and sprightliness of some of Turgenev's heroines, and her reverie when as an old woman she drives through the moonlit countryside to her husband's death-bed has something of the Turgenev atmosphere. Unfortunately Bennett tries to achieve his "syntheticimpressionism" (as he calls it in his *Journals*) by much the same methods that he employed, with far greater success, for "the envelope of facts": he accumulates his suggestive touches in the same way that he accumulates his concrete details, laying them one on top of the other like so many bricks, so that the cracks between them are always visible. There is none of the perfect fusion of elements, the natural shapeliness, that, in spite of his complaints of a lack of "architecture" mark Turgenev's work.

Bennett's calm assumption that he has "picked up" Turgenev's technical devices, as if they were items listed in a writer's handbook, is in fact on a par with other professions of a similar nature —that he would use the "tone" of Tolstoy's *Death of Ivan Ilych* (1886) in *The Old Wives' Tale*, for example, or that the final sequences of *War and Peace* have given him "a good basic scheme" for *These Twain* (1916). But this is merely to say that Turgenev has been "the novelists' novelist" for those who are incapable of benefiting from the relationship as well as for those who are.

John Galsworthy: 1867–1933

In the case of John Galsworthy we are once again dealing not with a case of mere lip-service to a passing fashion but with a deep and abiding influence. Ford Madox Ford had every justification when he wrote "I must have asked myself a hundred times in my life, if there had been no Turgenev, what would have become of Galsworthy . . . what would Galsworthy have become?"

What his admirers were quite sure he had *not* become was a materialist. To many of them he seemed just the opposite. André Chevrillon, for example, saw him as "a philosopher and a poet, a mystic poet", concerned with "the whole of reality", not only that which "ordinary eyes perceive", but also "the deeper spiritual reality". And Galsworthy himself proclaimed that

"the finality that is requisite to Art . . . is not the finality of dogma, not the finality of fact, it is ever the finality of feeling—

of a spiritual light, subtly gleaned by the spectator out of that queer luminous haze which one man's nature must ever be to others".

For what he meant by Realism in fiction was something very different from what Virginia Woolf attributed to him. It was in fact the kind of fiction that Turgenev wrote. When for example in "Vague Thoughts on Art" (*The Inn of Tranquillity*, 1924) he asks himself "What is Realism?" the immediate response is to cite the example of Turgenev, "the greatest poet ever to write in prose", and at the same time a poet who, more clearly than any other writer, "brought the actual shapes of men and things before us". Turgenev in fact represented for him the high water mark in the art of fiction. In "Six Novelists in Profile" (*Candelabra*, 1932) he argued that the Novel in the hands of Jane Austen, Dickens, Balzac, Stendhal, Thackeray and Hugo (a curious alignment) had attained "a certain relation of part to whole". But it was left to

"one of more poetic feeling and greater sensibility than any of these to perfect its proportions and introduce the principle of selection, until there was that complete relation of part to whole which goes to the making of what we call a work of art".

The great weakness of the English Novel, he argued, was that it was inclined to self-indulgence, it often "went to bed drunk". And in his view whatever "niceness of deportment and proportion" it had achieved in recent years it owed in the main to Turgenev.

He deplored the "literary fashion" (according to his calculation it began in 1907) of disparaging Turgenev because "a new Russian lamp" had been discovered in Dostoyevsky. He defended him against his Russian critics, arguing that they had attacked him on political grounds because "he had a bad habit; he told the truth". He contrasted him in one of the letters with "the loose jointed giant Gogol" and "the shapeless giant Dostoyevsky". The *Brothers Karamazov* struck him as "amazing in places" —but "what incoherence and what verbiage and what startling of monsters out of holes to make you shudder", a sign it seemed to him of the "cubistic, blood-bespattered poster times". He contrasted him too with that "large violent being" Tolstoy, whose

H

method was "an infinity of fact and pictorial detail", and the very "opposite of Turgenev's which relied on selection and concentration, on atmosphere and poetic balance".

There is no doubt that Galsworthy's admiration for Turgenev as an artist sprang from a certain similarity in their situations, leading to a genuine temperamental affinity. They were both gentlemen with inheritances : they were both expensively educated, cultured, fond of travel and of sport. They both found themselves out of step with their own class, critical of its traditions and conventions, but still rooted in it, so that both of them frequently harked back to a golden age of patrician virtue—Galsworthy, for example, in *The Portrait*, and Turgenev in his various idealized portraits of old-world landowners. They were both sensitive to the injustices inflicted on the victims of the social system, but were both unable to throw themselves whole-heartedly into a cause. They were both, therefore, torn between conflicting loyalties, and —once again—fundamentally exiles. Both writers, too, in reaction against the traditions of their class, abandoned the faith of their fathers, and sought refuge from their sense of isolation in a philosophy blended of agnosticism, humanism, stoicism and a slightly ironic fatalism. But at the same time they were both unable to turn to the extreme of materialism : their sense of loss was therefore further intensified, and in both cases the resultant mood was one of gentle, resigned melancholy which found expression in evocative, pastel-shaded descriptions of Nature. And both writers projected their dilemmas into fictional terms, creating heroes of roughly the same stamp—though Mr. Frank Swinnerton (in *The Georgian Literary Scene*, 1935) summed up the difference in the stature of their genius with his caustic comment "Turgenev was at bottom a poet, Galsworthy at heart a gentleman".

The first of Galsworthy's novels, on his own testimony, to be directly inspired by Turgenev was *Villa Rubein* (1900). What he had primarily derived from him, he believed, was "an insight into proportion of theme and economy of words", and he felt that *Villa Rubein* as a result was "more genuine, more atmospheric", and better balanced. Turgenev's influence, however, is not only apparent in the technique, which certainly shows a marked improvement on that of the early tales, written under the pseudonym of John Sinjohn. There are in fact numerous echoes from his reading of Turgenev.

The central situation for example is very close to that of Turgenev's novels. Christian is a pure, idealistic girl, gently nurtured but, like Turgenev's heroines, full of fire and independence. Like Elena in *On the Eve* she accepts the great challenge of her life calmly and courageously, defying the wishes of her father and the conventions of the society in which she has been brought up. As with Elena the romantic, generous elements in her nature respond to the demands made upon it by her lover's fanatical devotion to a cause—in this case not to the dangers and sufferings of political action but to the insecurity of Bohemianism.

Alois Harz himself is a curious mixture of Bohemian, Nihilist and Galsworthy gentleman-at-heart. He has the single-mindedness of Insarov, and just as Insarov is prepared to run away from Elena because he fears his love for her may distract him from his political devotion, so Alois decides to leave Christian for fear she may interfere with his painting. And both of them have reckoned without their lovers' determination and capacity for sacrifice.

It is the name of Bazarov, however, that most frequently crops up in the letters that passed to and fro between Galsworthy, Edward Garnett, Ford Madox Ford, and Joseph Conrad at this period—and there are some respects in which Harz recalls the hero of *Fathers and Children*. His attitude towards his art is as proud and sternly self-dedicated as Bazarov's towards his science. Like him he has had to struggle against poverty, like him he comes of humble origins—and the visit he makes to his parents in their cottage home recalls that of Bazarov to his parents. Like Bazarov too he despises cant, weakness, hypocrisy, and privilege. And finally the "Villa Rubein" itself, with its representatives of different families and generations concentrated under one roof, inevitably recalls the various "nests of gentlefolk" in Turgenev.

Most of the other tales of the period also bear witness to what he admitted in his Nobel Prize speech was a thorough soaking in Maupassant—and Turgenev. *First Love* (1860) and *The Torrents of Spring* in particular seem to have affected him. In each of these stories an elderly or middle-aged man recalls an emotional experience of his youth which, in retrospect, appears as the turning-point of his whole life; and the use of the "flash-back" in each case serves to heighten the poignancy and the sense of irreparable loss. It is an approach of which Galsworthy was particularly fond. In *The Salvation of a Forsyte* (1900), for example, Swithin, as he lies on his death-bed, remembers the one romantic episode in his life.

Some of the details of this story recall *On the Eve*. Boleskey, the Hungarian nationalist for example reminds one of Insarov, and Rozsi his daughter, in her devotion to her father's cause, has something in common with Elena. Boleskey's quarrel with the Austrian officers in the café also suggests Insarov's encounter with the Germans during the excursion to Tsaritsina.

But it also echoes Sanin's chivalrous championship of Gemma in the inn garden outside Frankfort; Count Kasteliz's jealousy of Swithin also recalls Herr Klüber's. The relationship to *Torrents of Spring* is in fact particularly close. The central situation is very similar. Thus in Turgenev's tale the hero, swept off his feet by Gemma's enchantment, is caught up in a strange milieu far from his native land, until his encounter with his fellow countryman Polozov eventually leads to his desertion of Gemma. Swithin too finds himself torn between the conditioning of his class and upbringing, and the fascination of Rozsi and the strange and exciting way of life she represents—until the memory of his twin brother James, waiting for him to continue a conventional Englishman's continental holiday, finally causes him to abandon her. And, like Sanin, Swithin at the end of the tale is filled with regret, realizing too late that he had turned his back on what mattered most in life . . . "Aloud in his sleep Swithin muttered, 'I've missed it!' . . ."

Although Galsworthy believed that *Villa Rubein* was "more genuine, more atmospheric, better balanced", he was still, he confessed in *The Triad* (1924), dissatisfied. The "real tug of war", he tells us, began with *The Pagan*, which underwent two rewritings on the advice of Edward Garnett and eventually emerged as *The Island Pharisees* in 1904. It is certainly his first really unified work of fiction, and it is far from being a typical sprawling Edwardian family novel. In many ways it is not a novel at all, but a series of scenes or sketches, each of which demonstrates some particular aspect of Island Pharisaism—the Country House, the University, the Army, the Indian Civil Service and so

on. It is saved from being a mere thesis with illustrations, however, by the consistency of temper which provides impetus and
tension and by the tautness and economy of the structure as a
whole.

The underlying mood of the novel derives only indirectly from
Turgenev. For it is also the outcome of his personal experience of
ostracism, and here and there a personal bitterness breaks
through. As, for example, when Shelton overhears a group of
Island Pharisees discussing the case of one of their number who,
like Galsworthy himself, had broken the social code.

"You can't tell *what* a fellow'll do," he makes Maby say,
"take to drink or writin' books."

The gradual process of disillusionment and self-discovery that
takes place in Shelton's mind is reflection of Galsworthy's own
painful adjustment to the fact that he cannot belong to his own
kind, a particularly painful process because, as with Rudin and
Nezhdanov, the secret yearning for conformity and "belonging"
is as strong as the instinct for revolt.

From the more general technical and aesthetic point of view,
however, Turgenev's influence dominated the writing of *The
Island Pharisees*. We know from the letters that he was in the
forefront of Galsworthy's mind, and that his friends were continually urging his example upon him, and the book was in fact
dedicated to Constance Garnett in gratitude for her translations
from Turgenev. Various aspects of Turgenev's characterizations
too have found their way into the novel. The portrait of Shelton
certainly owes a good deal to some of his heroes. He does not,
like Nezhdanov and Dmitri Rudin, try to signalize his rebellion
against his own class by "going to the people" : he is still in the
process of disillusionment—though his relationship with Ferrand
the vagabond fulfils something of the same function. He is like
them however in so far as he is the typically nineteenth-century
Liberal "gentleman with a conscience", and many of his self-com-
munings recall theirs. He is more like Rudin perhaps than
Nezhdanov, who is more bashful (and less aristocratic) than
either, and his probings and comments have more of Rudin's
intensity.

Once again, however, it is the presence of Bazarov which
makes itself most strongly felt. Thus Ferrand strikes Shelton as

having that "air of knowing and being master of his fate" which is one of Bazarov's outstanding characteristics, and he has in consequence the power of disturbing his peace of mind, just as Bazarov does that of Arkady. Ferrand's presence in the Dennant household, too, is clearly modelled on that of Bazarov at Maryino, and it has much the same disruptive effect. Like Bazarov he scornfully resists any attempts to civilize or to patronize him, and he too, Galsworthy tells us, "stood for discontent with the accepted". The difference between them is that Ferrand, unlike Bazarov, is at heart a vagabond : he is an Anarchist rather than a Nihilist—or one might apply to him the paradox that he is a Nihilist without a purpose. But though he is softer than Bazarov, there is an unmistakable family resemblance.

Some of Bazarov's qualities have also found their way into Shelton, who is certainly no naïve Arkady : his attitude towards accepted shibboleths can be as devastating as that of Bazarov himself and his habit of Socratic questioning often recalls Bazarov's inquisitions of the brothers Kirsanov. His relationship with Antonia too has a certain resemblance to that of Bazarov with Anna Sergyevna, in so far as in both cases the passion is a hopeless one in view of the ideological gulf that separates the men from the women they love.

Shelton's relationship with Antonia is indeed one of the most successful elements in the book, and the one which largely saves it from being a mere tract in social disillusionment. It symbolizes the intellectual and spiritual ferment taking place in his mind, almost as poignantly as does the lake for George Moore's Father Oliver. And as in so many of Galsworthy's novels the evocation of young love owes much to Turgenev. Knowing as we do that Turgenev was constantly in his mind during the writing of *The Island Pharisees*, it is possible, quite apart from the general similarity of tone and atmosphere, to detect specific echoes. Behind the scene in the garden, for example, when Antonia loads Shelton with the flowers she has been picking, we can sense the presence of Gemma and her cherries. The glimpse that Shelton catches at the dinner-party of the "white gleam" of Antonia's dress across the lawn, is a faint echo from Lavretsky's moonlight encounters with Lisa, and here too it is noticeable that Galsworthy like Turgenev uses the natural background, and the impending storm, to reflect the mood of the protagonists. Antonia herself has something of Lisa's youthful innocence and charm, and her subservience to her milieu is not without its pathos.

The presence of Bazarov can be felt in another of the earlier novels. In his portrait of Lord Miltoun in *The Patrician* (1911) Galsworthy has transposed the class and the setting, but Bazarov's pride, force of personality, fixity of purpose, and integrity, his power of shocking the comfortable, whether friend or foe, are all in evidence. Miltoun's liaison with Mrs. Noel also suggests Bazarov's passion for Anna Sergyevna (though it also has more than a touch of Pinero and the drama of High Society). The inference is moreover once again borne out by the correspondence. Conrad, for example, writing to Galsworthy just after the publication of *The Patrician*, described Miltoun as "a very consistently sombre figure" who stood out from the other characters in the book in "a very striking manner".

> "He is to my mind," Conrad added, "more sombre than Bazarov, and almost as plebeian, with his temperamental asceticism, his Nonconformist conscience, and his passion. . . . He is a strange bird to come out of that nest."[1]

In *Thus to Revisit* (1921) Ford Madox Ford suggested that the "earnest student of Turgenev" was in his later work somewhat "overwhelmed" by the "more purposeful sociologist and philanthropist". But this is rather to miss the point of Turgenev's influence. For Turgenev also helped Galsworthy to create a portrait gallery of contemporary types, who would illustrate the forces at work in society. It must be remembered that many of Galsworthy's types, and hence many of his themes, are similar in substance and treatment to Turgenev's. Most of his upper-class "do-gooders"—Gregory Vigil in *The Country House* (1907) for example—bear a distinct family resemblance to Turgenev's reformers, though both their revolutionary ardour and their "Hamletism" are weaker, and indeed both Edward Garnett and Conrad urged the examples of Rudin and Nezhdanov upon him. Galsworthy, moreover, like Turgenev, makes his rebels an integral

---

[1] Conrad's use of the word "nest" is obviously a reference to Turgenev's *A Nest of Gentlefolk*.

part of the world of the country house: they are in revolt against it, but fundamentally they belong to it—just as the "fast" county types, the Bellews in *The Country House*, for example, belong to it in spite of their outlawry. In a sense indeed the revolt of both these types is a guarantee of the existing social order rather than a threat to it—they act as often as not as safety-valves, or Dreadful Warnings. There is certainly no sense of impending revolution in Galsworthy, in spite of the characters' occasional violence of speech or action, and Turgenev's studies of social ferment in fact constituted less of a threat to the existing order than Tolstoy's drastic spiritual and ethical challenges, or Chekhov's exposure of inner decay. The point is, perhaps, that they were both studying a society which was at a slightly earlier stage—a society just before the crisis, in the "last phase but one" before the inevitable collapse set in, the stage at which the clash of loyalties and of generations particularly occurs. But above all Galsworthy studied the ways in which Turgenev turned his social figures into living men and women, softening the outlines of the type by a penumbra of atmosphere, bestowing humanity upon them through the complications of love and passion, and giving them depth and mystery by setting them against the backgrounds of Nature.

The most thorough-going instance of his discipleship to Turgenev is provided, among the tales, by *The Apple Tree* (1916). In form it is closely modelled on *The Torrents of Spring* and *First Love*. Like both of these it is a story within a story, using the technique of the flash-back. Thus Frank Ashurst sitting by the suicide's grave, which he has chanced on during his Devon motor tour, suddenly feels the ache of recollection: like Sanin when he comes across the garnet cross in a drawer of his desk, he has "stumbled on a buried memory, a wild sweet time, swiftly choked . . . and ended. And turning on his face, he rested his chin on his hands. . . . And this is what he remembered . . ."

When we are back in the long forgotten love-story, the echoes from Turgenev come thick and fast. As far as atmosphere is concerned the tale is almost a pastiche of borrowings from Turgenev. The description of Ashurst's state of mind after his first meeting with Megan, for example, reproduces the very texture of the emotion experienced by the young narrator of *First Love*. Similarly his rendezvous with Megan in the moonlit orchard, with its lyrical, rapturous atmosphere, is strongly reminiscent of similar trysts in Turgenev—that of Insarov with Elena, for example, or that of Lavretsky with Lisa. Ashurst's vigil outside Megan's window too recalls that of Lavretsky outside Lisa's, and his return to the same spot years later suggests, even more forcibly, Lavretsky's sad revisiting of the garden where he and Lisa had discovered each other's love.

> "He . . . began pacing up and down over the grass, a grey phantom coming to substance for a moment in the light from the lamp at either end. He was with her again under the living, breathing whiteness of the blossom . . . back in the rapture of his kisses on her upturned face of innocence and humble passion ; back in the suspense and beauty of that pagan night. He stood still once more in the shadow of the lilacs."

By comparison with Turgenev it is over-done—as is the melodramatic ending of the tale when Ashurst discovers that the suicide's grave upon which he has been reclining is that of Megan herself. Turgenev's unique greatness lay in his power of conjuring up mood and atmosphere by the most subtle and economical of means, by reducing description to a minimum, and by making the characters themselves reveal the scene to us. This perfect fusion of word and act, character and background was beyond Galsworthy's powers, but it was the ideal towards which he continually worked.

The Apple Tree is as close to Turgenev in theme as it is in atmosphere. The liaison between gentleman and peasant girl is one of Turgenev's basic themes, and he handles it with kindness, and delicacy—as in the relationship between Nikolai Petrovitch and Fenitchka in *Fathers and Children*. The undergraduate smugness of Ashurst is more reminiscent of the insufferable valet, Viktor, in *The Tryst*, one of the stories in *A Sportsman's Sketches*, which has undoubtedly influenced *The Apple Tree*.

Akulina, the serf girl heroine of this tale, is clearly the prototype of Megan. Turgenev's description of her (in the rôle of compassionate witness), "I was especially taken with the expression of her face, it was so simple and gentle, so sad and so full of childish wonder at its own sadness", sets the tone for Galsworthy's more laboured descriptions of Megan. And Megan's pathetic devotion to Ashurst follows closely that of Akulina. When, for example, Viktor condescendingly pats Akulina's shoulder, she seizes his hand and covers it with kisses, and Megan too snatches at Ashurst's hand and presses it to "her cheek, her heart, her lips". A little later, like Akulina, she lies at her lover's feet—though Turgenev, with his usual artistic reticence, spares us the distasteful addition of her seeking to kiss them. And her cry of despair "I shall die if I can't be with you" echoes that of Akulina.

In the working out of the plot itself, however, Galsworthy has drawn chiefly on *The Torrents of Spring*. There are many small details which correspond closely. Thus Ashurst, when he feels Megan's heart "beating against him" knows "to the full the sensations of chivalry and passion. Because she was not of his world, because she was simple and young and headlong, adoring and defenceless, how could he be other than her protector?" Sanin too congratulates himself on his chivalry in deciding to marry Gemma, although she is "not of his world".

Ashurst too, like Sanin, leaves his betrothed on what is, at the outset, intended to be a temporary absence in order to make arrangements for the promised marriage. Like Sanin he unexpectedly encounters an old friend, one who really does "belong to his world", and in his case as in Sanin's this chance meeting marks the beginning of his betrayal. For like Sanin Ashurst becomes involved with his old friend, takes up old ties and interests and enters thoroughly into his old milieu. He finds himself attracted to Stella just as Sanin finds himself drawn to the more sinister temptress Maria Nikolaevna. He sends vague excuses for his prolonged absence to Megan just as Sanin does to Gemma, and he finds it impossible to break away from the Hallidays, just as Sanin, for rather more subtle reasons, cannot disentangle himself from the Polozovs, and like Sanin he shirks personal explanations and simply abandons his sweetheart. His chance encounter with Megan while he is driving in the landau with the Hallidays recalls that of Sanin with Pantaleone and Emilio in Paris while he is driving with the Polozovs, and like Sanin (successfully in his case) he tries to hide himself from view. At the end of the story Ashurst's return to the scene of his love reminds one of Sanin's return to Frankfort, and like Sanin

Ashurst is now seized by "an ache for lost youth, a hankering, a sense of wasted love and sweetness".

As far as the *Forsyte Saga* is concerned, it is Tolstoy's influence perhaps which is the more important. But the earlier books in the series (before the concept of a Saga had properly emerged) were written while Galsworthy was still undergoing his apprenticeship to Turgenev, and in *The Triad* he seems to suggest that this was especially so in the case of *The Man of Property* (1906). Turgenev in fact continued to be his model in matters of structure and proportion, and often in technique.

Irene's situation is so close to that of Anna Karenina, however, that the elements in her character that are derived from Turgenev have been overlooked. In fact she has really more in common with Turgenev's heroines than with Tolstoy's. She has much of the grace, tenderness and candour of Lisa in *A Nest of Gentlefolk* or of Katya in *Fathers and Children*. She is made to stand out against the Forsyte background just as Turgenev's heroines rise above the conventions and standards of the way of life in which they have been reared. Like them she embodies the deeper human and spiritual values which are in danger of being overthrown by Sipyagins and Nezhdanovs alike. Galsworthy's preoccupation throughout the Saga was, he tells us in the Preface, to illustrate the "impingement of Beauty and the claims of Freedom" on the Forsyte scheme of values, and Irene herself he envisaged as "a concretion of disturbing Beauty impinging on a possessive world". And the emotional tone, the whole atmosphere with which he surrounds her, derives from Turgenev's heroines rather than from Tolstoy's adulteress.

This is particularly noticeable perhaps in *Indian Summer of a Forsyte* (1918). The mood of this book is very close to that of the final sequence of *A Nest of Gentlefolk*, and old Jolyon as he sits in the garden at Robin Hill with his beloved grandchildren near at hand reminds one of Lavretsky when in later life he revisits Lisa's old home, and sits musing on the garden seat while the young people play in the background. For Lavretsky the garden is impregnated with the poignancy of his lost love : we feel the presence of Lisa like a ghost. And Robin Hill too is haunted by the love of Bosinney and Irene.

Old Jolyon's mood, like Lavretsky's, is one of resignation

tinged by regret for lost opportunities, though the tragedy of course is not his tragedy, and the regret in consequence is neither so painful nor so poignant. In Turgenev, moreover, there is always that other dimension provided by the consciousness of great issues lurking in the background which gives depth to so much of Russian fiction—for Lavretsky is not only the victim of a tragic love affair, he is also the representative of a whole frustrated generation. But in spite of the differences there is a real kinship between the two. The closing sequence of *The Indian Summer of a Forsyte* in particular recalls in atmosphere that of *A Nest of Gentlefolk*. Thus Old Jolyon falls into his last sleep in the garden at Robin Hill:

> ". . . Some thistledown came on what little air there was, and pitched on his moustache, more white than itself. He did not know; but his breathing stirred it, caught there. A ray of sunlight struck through and lodged on his boot. A humble bee alighted and strolled on the crown of his Panama hat. And the delicious surge of slumber reached the brain beneath that hat, and the head swayed forward and rested on his breast. Summer—summer! So went the hum.
>
> "The stable clock struck the quarter past. The dog Balthasar stretched and looked up at his master. The thistledown no longer moved. The dog placed his chin over the sunlit foot. It did not stir, the dog withdrew his chin quickly, rose, and leaped on old Jolyon's lap, looked in his face, whined; then, leaping down, sat on his haunches gazing up. And suddenly he uttered a long, long howl.
>
> "But the thistledown was still as death, and the face of his old master.
>
> "Summer—summer—summer! The soundless footsteps on the grass."

This is close to the poignant tone and atmosphere of Lavretsky's reverie:

> "Lavretsky went out of the house into the garden, and sat down on the familiar garden seat. And on this loved spot facing the house . . . he a solitary homeless wanderer, looked

back upon his life, while the joyous shouts of the younger
generation who were already filling his place, floated across
the garden to him. . . . His heart was sad, but not weighed
down nor bitter; much there was to regret, nothing to be
ashamed of.

"'Play away, be gay, grow strong, vigorous youth!' he
thought, and there was no bitterness in his meditations; 'your
life is before you, and your life will be easier; you have not,
as we had, to find out a path for ourselves, to struggle, to fall
and to rise again in the dark; we had enough to do to last out
—and how many of us did last out?—but you need only to do
your duty, work away, and the blessing of an old man be with
you. For me, after today, after these emotions, there remains
to take my leave at last—and though sadly, without envy,
without any dark feelings, to say, in sight of the end, in sight
of God who awaits me 'Welcome lonely old age! burn out
useless life!'"

It is even more interesting, however, to consider this passage
from *A Nest of Gentlefolk* in relation to another novelist—one
who, though he was a friend of Galsworthy, would undoubtedly have approached the task of depicting Mrs. Brown
in the spirit which Virginia Woolf considered proper for the
twentieth-century novelist.

JOSEPH CONRAD: 1856–1924

Critics have tended to place a false emphasis on the Russian
influence in the work of Joseph Conrad. The distortion arose
largely because his advent more or less coincided with the
Russian fever. Critics have a curious habit of assuming that they
know more about a writer's intentions than he does himself: they
were determined that Conrad should have a Slav Soul on the
Dostoyevsky pattern and dismissed his own hostility towards
Dostoyevsky on the ground that he was leaning over backwards
to deny the Slav element in his nature.

It is true that he did not like the Slav label, and his dislike of
Dostoyevsky and Tolstoy may have been in part prompted by

anti-Russian feeling, and the desire to assert his "Western" affiliations. But there seems no good reason to disbelieve his own statement (in a letter to Edward Garnett, May 1917) that he was not at all qualified "to speak on things Russian", and that he knew no Russian. There had been no soaking himself in Russian literature in his youth, he insisted. As a boy he remembered reading *Smoke* in a Polish translation, and *A Nest of Gentlefolk* in French—and liking them "purely by instinct". But it was not until many years later that he gave them any more serious consideration—not in fact until he met Edward Garnett. "It was *you*," he wrote, "who have opened my eyes to the value and quality of Turgenev." And like all the other contemporary English novelists he came to Turgenev through the translations of Constance Garnett.

> "Turgenev for me is Constance Garnett and Constance Garnett *is* Turgenev," he wrote—"she has done that marvellous thing of placing the man's work inside English literature, and it is there that I see it—or rather that I *feel* it."

He felt it, moreover, almost completely divorced from Slav politics or Slav psychology. It was left to Edward Garnett, he believed, to see Turgenev "not only in relation to mankind, but in his relation to Russia". For his own part he was not interested in Turgenev's Russian-ness. In his approach to him he regarded Russia as no more "than the canvas to the painter. If his people all lived on the moon he would have been just as great an artist. They are very much like Shakespeare's Italians. One doesn't think of it."

It is not in fact a matter of a Slav element or a French element or an English element, but of a way of looking at life and his relation to it as an artist. He regarded Tolstoy and Dostoyevsky from the standpoint of the kind of artist he was, and rejected them neither because he disliked their nationality, nor because he was repressing a secret kinship, but simply because their vision of life as artists was not to his purpose.

That he was exercising this kind of discrimination is indeed made clear by the tenor of his attacks on them. In the letter to Edward Garnett, for example, he speaks, with reference to

Dostoyevsky, of "the grimacing, haunted creature" who is most likely to throw the critics into hysterical transports while they turn their backs on the virtues of a Turgenev—"for you know, my dear Edward, that if you were to catch Antinous and exhibit him in a booth of the world's fair, swearing that his life was as perfect as his form" the crowd would be "struggling next door to catch a sight of the double-headed nightingale, or of some weak kneed giant grinning through a collar".

And it is here that the description of Lavretsky's frame of mind at the end of *A Nest of Gentlefolk* can be seen as particularly relevant to Conrad's own view of life. In his letter to Edward Garnett he suggests that the main reason why "in the longer, non-Russian view" Turgenev should be "sympathetic and welcome to the English speaking world" is his "essential humanity" —the fact that all his characters, "fortunate and unfortunate, oppressed and oppressors, are human beings", not as in Dostoyevsky, he implies, "strange beasts in a menagerie, or damned souls knocking themselves to pieces in the stuffy darkness of mystical contradictions", but "human beings fit to live, fit to suffer, fit to win, fit to lose, in the endless and inspiring game of pursuing from day to day the ever-receding future".

And again he makes his attitude perfectly clear in a letter to Galsworthy in which he points out to him that too didactic a purpose can be dangerous to a writer, leading to "a vain harrowing of our feelings", and at the worst (as he believes) to

"the gratuitous atrocity of say, 'Ivan Ilyitch' or the monstrous stupidity of such a thing as 'The Kreutzer Sonata' . . . where an obvious degenerate, not worth looking at twice, totally unfitted not only for married life but for any sort of life, is presented as a sympathetic victim of some sort of sacred truth that is supposed to live within him. . . ."

Conrad's own scheme of values is based on just such broad generalizations about courage, love, self-sacrifice, devotion to duty as are exemplified in the story of Lavretsky and Lisa. His passionate admiration for Turgenev springs from a deep sense of sympathy with the simple emotional and moral patterning of his tales and novels. He valued him because he too believed in courage and endurance, and because he too dealt with simple, uncomplicated love and passion in stories that did not probe into the darker places of the human psyche, but which, he was convinced, would "endure at least till the infinite emotions of love are replaced by the exact simplicity of perfected Eugenics".

The truth is that Conrad did not really have any profound philosophical message to offer, and he was not really interested in "psychology", in the sense that critics brought up on Dostoyevsky and Freud expected of him. Like Turgenev he was, as far as motivation was concerned, content with a handful of basic moral generalizations—such as are represented in his work by the Merchant Service, and by the peasants in Turgenev's *A Sportsman's Sketches*—though at the same time his morality, like Turgenev's, has a certain stamp of aristocratic dignity, concerned with a kind of antique virtue in the Roman sense. What he was *not* interested in, any more than Turgenev, was "analysis" of character.

But a novelist in order to be great does not *have* to be an analyst of character. His creations do not have to be convincing outside the books to which they belong. They do not have to be "true to life", and it is not even essential that the novelist should "understand" them in the psychological sense. Provided, that is, that he is aware of them, with all the sensibilities of original genius, provided that he makes them utterly convincing sensuously and spiritually within their own particular universe. It is this kind of genius that Conrad admired in Turgenev, and it is the kind of genius that he himself possessed.

To say that Tolstoy and Dostoyevsky *were* philosophical or psychological novelists, and very great ones, does not imply that they lacked this power of concrete realization—for we know that they possessed it to a supreme degree. But their main concern was to show, in profound and subtle detail, the motivations of their characters, and the processes taking place in their souls. The milieu in which they are placed, the atmosphere that surrounds them, for example, are directly related to these considerations, and are in fact reflections of the analysis of character.

In Turgenev too background, as we have seen, was intimately related to character, but in a different way. His characters are certainly convincing within their total context, but the relationship of milieu and background to character is a special one. The two continually interpenetrate each other, and yet they are "separate" in the sense that an image is separate from the thing it represents. Whereas it would be possible in Dostoyevsky to point to a scene as a direct and thrilling revelation of the state of mind of one of his characters, in Turgenev it would be necessary to indicate the two side by side. The relationship between scenes and states of mind in Dostoyevsky is, in spite of his apparent confusion and in spite of his mysticism, more direct than in Turgenev. Psychological interpretations, it is true, can be suggested for many of the famous scenes in his work too—but the connection is less explicit, it is, one might say, subconscious—and this is perhaps what Turgenev himself had in mind when he spoke of the novelist as a "secret psychologist".

This is however another way of saying that Turgenev's methods were closer to the fusion that takes place in poetry, so that background, action and utterance are all to some extent a kind of imagery. And this is equally true of Conrad. The reality and completeness he aims at, like those of Turgenev, are poetic and dramatic rather than psychological. This indeed becomes obvious on the occasions when the fusion fails to take place. Then the characters become bare and lifeless, the handful of simple heroic virtues is revealed as utterly inadequate, the language becomes overloaded and forced, and the whole suddenly sinks to the level of the magazine romance. Thus the characters in Conrad's *The Arrow of Gold* (1919) are puppets set against a series of unrelated purple passages: Insarov in *On the Eve* is a wooden figure because unlike the other characters in the book he is not thoroughly absorbed into the total context, and in some of Turgenev's tales the characters become mawkish, the situations banal and sentimental. Even in their greatest work the characters remain comparatively simple, and we are often reminded, particularly in the case of Conrad, of Dickens' two-dimensional creations. But they also take on the subtle and satisfying overtones of poetry, so that many of the tales of love, courage, and devotion become almost prototypes, like the figures of the ancient myths and fables which present in crystallized form the basic human instincts. It is for this reason that a tale like *Mumu* is a universal expression of oppression, just as *First Love* is a

I

universal symbol of its subject, and *The Torrents of Spring* the summation of all regret for vanished youth. It is in this sense that Conrad saw Turgenev as Shakespearian, and it is the sense in which Conrad himself was Shakespearian.

It is at this level that Turgenev's "influence" on Conrad must be discussed. He was too original a writer to need to copy techniques, themes, or situations—which proceeded from the only authentic source, his own creative imagination working upon his personal experience. But here and there the more superficial evidences of his study of Turgenev are also apparent. They are most obvious perhaps in the early *Almayers Folly* (1895). Mr. Richard Curle, for example, has pointed out the similarity between Markelov's moods of sombre irritability in *On the Eve*, and those of the sullen, resentful Almayer and the atmosphere of stultifying intrigue in this novel probably owes something to Turgenev's *Smoke*. The real prototype of Almayer, however, is Rudin—and Almayer is a kind of decayed Rudin whose nobility has fallen from him.

The Rudin-Nezhdanov character type recurs fairly frequently, in *Lord Jim* (1906), and in *Victory* (1915), for example. Bazarov perhaps has lent a touch to the make-up of Nostromo, while many of Conrad's women, in their sensibility and integrity, in their passionate sense of duty, in the simple spontaneous nature of their love, remind one of Turgenev's heroines.

Ford Madox Ford has also drawn a comparison between Razumov's hopeless love for Nathalie Haldin in *Under Western Eyes* (1911), and that of Lavretsky for Lisa. A large part of the case for Dostoyevsky's influence on Conrad rests on this novel and certainly Conrad makes use of some of the Dostoyevskyan devices, for purposes of his own, as we shall see later. But Ford was right in speaking of Turgenev as the real shaping presence behind the book. Nathalie Haldin, for example, is closer to Turgenev's heroines than to Dostoyevsky's, while Conrad's portrayal of revolutionary society abroad, with its ironical overtones and antitheses, derives from Turgenev's descriptions of similar circles in *Smoke* rather than from anything in Dostoyevsky. The use of the English teacher as narrator, which contributes to the ironical control, is also more suggestive of Turgenev's techniques.

To speak of the irony of Turgenev and Conrad is to force us to look again at the apparent simplicity of their characters. True they represent a stern, old-fashioned morality, but there is nothing boy-scoutish about Conrad's merchant seamen, any more than there is about Turgenev's peasants. There is no heartiness, no inherent optimism in their outlook. On the contrary one suspects that the simple scheme of moral values was for both writers something of a personal necessity—that at times it was all that lay between them and a void. And perhaps the really deep kinship lies in an ever-present sense of isolation and emptiness—what Conrad meant by the "real horror" of *The Heart of Darkness* (1902). It derives, not from any mythical Slav Soul, but from a deep psychological conditioning which they shared in common, and which we have seen operating too in some of the other cases we have studied. For Conrad too was like Turgenev an exile, in an actual as well as a psychological sense, just as many of their characters—in Turgenev, Rudin, Nezhdanov, the narrator of *The Diary of a Superfluous Man*, the members of the Russian colony at Baden-Baden, and Lavretsky; and in Conrad Almayer, Lord Jim, Heyst, Razumov, Captain Anthony, and Dr. Monygham—are exiles or outcasts.

This preoccupation with the outcast is itself a reflection of a deep personal sense of alienation, which is in both writers always toppling on the verge of a far-reaching scepticism. For the most part it is held at bay by the simple gospels of courage, love and duty. Sometimes it issues in a sudden glimpse of the horror of death. Thus when Conrad comments on Schonberg's infatuation in *Victory*—

"Forty five is the age of recklessness for many men, as if in defiance of the decay and death waiting with open arms in the sinister valley at the bottom of the inevitable hill. For every age is fed on illusions, lest men should renounce life early and the human race come to an end"

—he is speaking in his own voice and the tone is reminiscent of Turgenev's feeling, which he frequently expressed in his letters, that the glory of life belongs to a mythical youth, and that life was in reality over at thirty. Turgenev's scepticism which, as we have seen, upset many of his admirers, is always present not far below the surface. Even Lavretsky's brave demeanour on the garden seat is not without its touch of despair ("Welcome, lonely old age ! Burn out, useless life !"). Even in the portrayal of Elena's heroism in *On the Eve* there is the underlying suggestion of its futility. *First Love* and *The Torrents of Spring* are impregnated with the sense of loss, of "fallings from us, vanishings". And even in the most straightforward of Conrad's romances, "the horror and the emptiness" are lurking. The consciousness of their presence is in both writers the source of much of their strength: from it springs the strange suggestiveness, the power of evoking unseen forces and the irony and tension apparent in such antitheses as that between Bazarov and Arkady in *Fathers and Children*, or between Verloc and Winnie in *The Secret Agent* (1907). And in what is perhaps Conrad's greatest novel *Nostromo* (1904) it is felt more deeply and employed with more terrible effect than in Turgenev, for we are brought face to face with the fear that the Nihilism of Decoud is in fact stronger than the power of human love as represented by Mrs. Gould, or the simple, heroic virtue of Giorgio Viola the old Garibaldini, stronger even than the magnificent presence of "snow clad Higuerota".

VIRGINIA WOOLF: 1882–1941

Turgenev, then, cast his spell upon novelists whose approach to the problem of presenting Mrs. Brown differed very widely. But what of his relationship to Virginia Woolf herself?

At first sight we should be tempted to say that it simply did not exist. When in fact she published "The Russian Point of View" Galsworthy expressed his disappointment that she had made no mention of Turgenev. There is little doubt of course that she was reading the Russians quite early in her career as a novelist. But when she made her break with the old fictional conventions it was Dostoyevsky and Chekhov who were in the forefront of her mind, and it was under their "influence" (again the word needs inverted commas where marked originality of genius is involved) that she set out to explore the "cloudy, yeasty, precious stuff, the soul", and to demonstrate her belief that life was "not a series of gig lamps symmetrically arranged" but a "luminous halo, a semi-transparent envelope surrounding us from the beginning of consciousness to the end". But in 1933 she made amends in an article which she contributed to the *Yale Review*.

Here she reveals that in re-exploring Turgenev she had come to the realization that there were certain elements in his work, lacking in the other Russians, or present to a lesser degree, which had a special relevance for her. She was now, for one thing, much more concerned with Form. She makes this quite clear in her Diary. In an entry for Wednesday, 16th August, 1933, she tells us that she has been "rubbing at the Pargiters" (published in 1937 as *The Years*) and "thinking oh Lord am I ever going to pull all that into shape. What a tremendous struggle it will be! I want to discover Form, having been reading Turgenev."

> "Form," she wrote, "is the sense that one thing follows another rightly. This is partly logic. Turgenev wrote and re-wrote. To clear the truth of the unessential. But Dostoevsky would say that everything matters. But one can't read Dostoevsky again. . . ."

And throughout the entry the rival methods of Turgenev and Dostoyevsky are set against each other:

> ". . . The essential thing in a scene is to be preserved. How do you know what this is? How do we know if the Dostoevsky form is better or worse than the Turgenev? It seems less permanent. Turgenev's idea that the writer states the essential and lets the reader do the rest. Dostoevsky to supply the reader with every possible help and suggestion. . . ."

She explores this question further in the essay, pointing out that though the form and symmetry of Turgenev's novels make them more satisfying than most, "curiously of our own time, undecayed and complete in themselves", he was not a great narrative novelist. Often indeed he told a story badly, with numerous "loops and circumlocutions". Yet he succeeded in creating an impression of amazing balance and delicacy, and gave us a "generalized, harmonized picture of life". And this was not only because his scope was so wide, embracing (as Henry James had pointed out) all classes of society, but above all because there was always (as so often in Conrad) some character at the centre of his stories from which a whole succession of emotions radiated. The beauty of his structure in fact derives, as in Conrad's best work, from the emotional unity, not from the "architecture". But his "ear for emotion was so fine that if he uses an abrupt contrast, or passes away from his people to a description of the sky or of the forest, all is held together by the truth of his insight". And it is for this reason, she points out, that Turgenev's novels are "not merely symmetrical but make us feel so intensely". For example his heroes and heroines "are among the few fictitious characters of whose love we are convinced. It is a passion of extraordinary purity and intensity."

In returning to his novels after a long absence, she feels, one might at first find them "a little thin, slight and sketch-like in texture"—but soon one realizes that "the scene has a size out of all proportion to its length. It expands in the mind and lies there giving off fresh ideas, emotions, and pictures much as a moment in real life will sometimes only yield its meaning long after it has passed." Thus when Turgenev's people talk they use the most natural of speaking voices, yet what they say is always unexpected, and the meaning goes on "long after the sound has stopped". And if, during some pause, we look out of the window "the emotion is returned to us, deepened, because it is given through another medium, by the trees or the clouds, by the barking of a dog, or the song of a nightingale".

Now all this has an obvious bearing on Virginia Woolf's own work. It is particularly apposite perhaps to *The Years*, upon which she was working at the time. On the superficial level we can see that she has indeed attempted to impose Form upon the novel. She achieves it by means of the chronological arrangement of the scenes, whereby the earlier years are spaced out in leisurely fashion, fall thick and fast around the period of the Great War, which marks the climax both of the family and the national story, swelling out again into an undifferentiated "Present Day". Certain of the characters too, Eleanor, Rose, Martin, Sarah, Kitty, much as they themselves shift and change, scurrying from one activity to another, act, as in Turgenev, as points of focus and serve to steady the total effect, keeping it impressionistic indeed but saving it from blurring. In much the same way the sequence of the pageant, confused though it is in itself, provides an organizing principle in another novel of the last phase—*Between the Acts* (1941)—and here too the heroine's consciousness is a centre which gives the whole shape and coherence.

In her later work too she sets out to achieve something of Turgenev's clarity, or what older critics would have called his classical purity.

> "No hot and personal feeling has made the emotion local and transitory," she wrote in her essay. "The man who speaks is not a prophet clothed with thunder, but a seer who tries to understand."

And there is more detachment, more of the attitude of "the rapt watcher" in both *The Years* and *Between the Acts* than in the earlier novels (whether they are better as works of fiction is a different matter). There is also less probing into the problems and motives of her characters: nothing to correspond, for example, to Mrs. Dalloway's agonizing self-examination, or to Rhoda's or Neville's cries of anguish in *The Waves* (1931).

All this is particularly relevant to *The Years*. But much of what she said about Turgenev in her essay is equally applicable to her earlier work, so much so indeed that one cannot help wondering whether she too, like Henry James and Conrad, had a natural affinity to Turgenev stronger than has been generally realized. After all she was, like him, a poet in fiction, but a poet of a special kind, and perhaps the most interesting passage of her essay is the analysis of the peculiarly complex task which Turgenev set himself. She points out the apparent contradiction in Turgenev's remark to a young writer that one cannot arrive at the correct expression by observation alone, because it must rise spontaneously from the subconscious depths—and in his insistence in other contexts that the writer must be a devoted and tireless observer. And yet, she realizes, there is no real contradiction. Turgenev was merely insisting that the novelist must be at one and the same time observer and interpreter. Many novelists are one or the other—but few, she feels, can combine "the fact and

the vision". It is what Turgenev does continually : in each of the
short chapters of his short books the observer is constantly
showing us the clear-cut details but the interpreter immediately
reveals that the details are not there for their own sake, and
indeed the processes of observation and interpretation are
simultaneous.

The consequence is that we are always "looking at the same
thing from different angles" and it is because the chapters contain
so many contrasts, she suggests, that they hold so much.

"On one and the same page we have irony and passion ;
the poetic and the commonplace ; the tap drips and a nightingale sings. And yet, though the scene is made up of contrasts,
it remains the same scene ; our impressions are all relevant to
each other."

But does not this also apply with remarkable aptness to
Virginia Woolf's own methods from *Jacob's Room* (1922) onwards ? For however hard she may be striving to capture the ebb
and flow of the Soul, there are always the vivid sharply observed
details which emerge with such startling clarity to reveal the
innermost thoughts and feelings of her characters. Just as Turgenev in *Virgin Soil* shows us Solomin's chamois leather gloves
with their stiff fingers, or tells us in *Fathers and Children* how
Bazarov packs his best trousers at the top of his case, so Virginia
Woolf gives us the needle and thread in *Mrs. Dalloway* (1925), the
paper cut-outs in *To the Lighthouse* (1927) or Bridget clanking the
pail and scraping the scales of the breakfast fish in *The Waves*.
It is the method moreover of "The Lives of the Obscure" (in
The Common Reader) and of so many of the essays in *The Death
of the Moth* (1942)—the method in fact that came most naturally
to her.

Turgenev's continual "looking at things from different angles"
meant moreover, she points out, that with the possible exceptions
of Bazarov in *Fathers and Children* and Harlov in *A Lear of the
Steppes* (which might incidentally be compared in some respects
to Hardy's *The Mayor of Casterbridge*), there are in his books no
really outstanding "characters" as nineteenth-century novelists
understood the term. The people in most of his tales "shade off

into each other, making, with all their variations, one subtle and profound type rather than several distinct and highly individu-alized men and women". And this again is true of her own work, not only in *The Years* where a whole family emerges rather than a series of individuals, a family which in its turn is typical of a whole way of life—but also in the earlier novels where the characters, while remaining themselves, "shade off into each other" to create an impression of the ceaseless flow of human life, which in spite of the myriad shapes and colours it assumes is always a single flow. Although the fortunes of the characters move us, the individual never dominates. As in Turgenev,

> "many other things seem to be going on at the same time. We hear the hum of life in the fields; a horse champs his bit; a butterfly circles and settles. And as we notice, without seeming to notice, life going on, we feel more intimately for the men and women themselves because they are not the whole of life, but only part of the whole. . . ."

Even to think about Turgenev, we see, impels her to the kind of creative writing that comes most naturally to her.

It is arguable, therefore, that though she excluded him from "The Russian Point of View", in the long run she found Turgenev the most sympathetic of all the Russian novelists. This may mean no more than that in many respects the two writers thought and felt alike about life and the problems of rendering it into fiction. But there can be no doubt that Turgenev was part of the intellectual climate in which she breathed, and it is at least clear that he was "the novelists' novelist" not only to the representatives of the older fiction such as Bennett and Galsworthy who would have devoted the great weight of their technique to Mrs. Brown's warts and wrinkles, but also to those "moderns" such as Conrad and Virginia Woolf herself who would have approached her fictional transmutation in a very different way.

CHAPTER EIGHT

THE ROUSSEAU OF HIS TIME

THE IMPACT OF TOLSTOY ON
ENGLISH THOUGHT AND FICTION

"IT IS not, perhaps, a strictly definable legacy; it is something in the air, a layer of the atmosphere," *The Times Literary Supplement* wrote in 1930, applying Plato's famous phrase to the Russian influence. This summing up, however, referred in particular to "the Russian fever", the period dominated by the great names of Tolstoy, Dostoyevsky and Chekhov, and fever is a condition which is certainly difficult to describe with any precision. It is this that justifies the amount of space which we have devoted to Turgenev, for though it may seem on the face of it to be disproportionate, the plain fact is that it is he who represents that part of the legacy which *is* most easily open to definition. In considering the rest of the legacy, in consequence, it will often be found that broad generalizations, usually involving considerations far removed from the literary, are often more profitable than the kind of study which we were justified in bringing to the admirers of "the novelists' novelist".

This is particularly true in the case of Tolstoy (1828 1910). The very magnitude of his genius, perhaps, repelled the more obvious sort of literary apprenticeship. He was, to use Bonamy Dobrée's phrase, "a man mountain", and the usual attitude towards him was one of awe.

This attitude, however, was inspired by Tolstoy the thinker as much as by Tolstoy the novelist. It was the social and religious writings that made the first real impact, and for some time the tendency was to keep the two aspects separate. Those who admired the artist deplored the increasing encroachments of the preacher. And on the other hand many who reverenced the preacher did not take much account of the artistic merits of the novels: even Matthew Arnold, who played such an important part in establishing Tolstoy's reputation in England, did not really regard *Anna Karenina* (1877) as a work of art. It was something different—a wonderful piece of reality, certainly of great moment for the status of the novel, but important chiefly in its moral implications. And the religious writings proper, particularly *My Religion* (or *What I Believe*, 1883–1884) which was translated in 1885 and which on the testimony of Havelock Ellis enjoyed a specially large circulation, aroused considerable interest before the novels were at all widely known, while the moral tales and fables appealed to a large public that either found the novels distasteful or did not even know of their existence.

The presence of Chertkov and his press in England, the first appearance of several of the pamphlets and articles in English, the visits of English and American admirers to Yasnya Polyana, the correspondence between Tolstoy and leading English and American thinkers, the setting up of the various Tolstoyan colonies, all helped to stimulate this kind of interest.

The impact throughout the world of Tolstoy's social and religious writings is a vast subject : here we can only touch upon a few of the more obvious aspects. It was undoubtedly one of the great events in the history of nineteenth-century thought, and one which cut across political and religious divisions. Thus George Bernard Shaw, with particular reference to *What is Art?* (1897), hailed "the voice of a master", and G. K. Chesterton declared "the Christianity of Tolstoy is, when we come to think of it, one of the most thrilling and dramatic incidents in our modern civilization".

He was often referred to as the Voltaire or the Rousseau of the nineteenth century. For if there was one element which more than any other explained the awe which Tolstoy inspired, it was his uncanny power of putting his finger exactly on those spots where the conscience of the West was most tender. The reaction of the average English reader of *What Then Must We Do?* (1886), for example, was summed up by *Temple Bar* in 1890—"One arises from its perusal no longer English or Russian, but a human being only, profoundly troubled, conscience-stricken. . . ."

In some respects indeed the English conscience was particularly sensitive to Tolstoy's teachings. His insistence, for example, that the moral law resides inside a man, and must be discovered (to use the English terminology) "by the light of reason" is really closer to English religious thinking than Dosto-yevsky's mysticism and his doctrine that God reveals Himself only through charity and pity. As Havelock Ellis triumphantly pointed out in *The New Spirit*—which was published in 1890 and which was one of the landmarks in the history of Tolstoy's reception in England—"He has nothing but contempt for 'faith', which he regards as merely a kind of lunacy."

However much, too, the English may have shrunk from Tolstoy's uncompromising attacks on accepted traditions and conventions, the Nonconformist, pamphleteering element in their own make-up could not fail to have a sneaking sympathy with his iconoclasm, and it is interesting to note that de Vogüé showed far less understanding of Tolstoy's personality in this respect than the average English commentator. His views on Art, and particularly his wilful attacks on many of the great names of the past, may have infuriated large numbers of his readers, but the revulsion was not without attraction. Some of Tolstoy's defenders, attempting to soften the blow, pointed out that his ideas would not strike his Russian readers as unusual because they belonged to a well-established tradition of Russian literary criticism. But indeed a similar tradition existed in England. It was a long time since Sir Philip Sidney had found it necessary to come to the defence of Poesy against the attacks of Stephen Gosson: Gosson was the spokesman nevertheless of deep-rooted instincts, and the tradition which he represented was itself part of the pattern of English thought and feeling. The nineteenth-century controversy between the advocates of Art for Art's sake and Art in the service of humanity was indeed, in many respects, a con-tinuation of the old dichotomy. There were powerful elements in contemporary English thought to whom Tolstoy's attitude would not fundamentally seem at all unreasonable. Thus George Bernard Shaw declared, according to *Table Talk* :

> "I have always been Puritan in my attitude to art. I am as fond of fine music and handsome buildings as Milton was, or Cromwell, or Bunyan; but if I found that they were becoming the instruments of a systematic idolatry of sensuous-ness, I would hold it good statesmanship to blow up every

cathedral in the world to pieces with dynamite, organ and all, without the least heed to the screams of the art critics and the cultured voluptuaries."

And in his review of *What is Art?* in the *Daily Chronicle* (September 10, 1898) he expressed his warm approval of the axiom that "Art is socially important . . . only in so far as it wields that power of propagating feeling" which Tolstoy sets up as "the criterion of true Art". There were many others, too, both in England and America, who, though they may have quarrelled with Tolstoy's individual assessments, were in general sympathy with his point of view. William Dean Howells, for example, found himself in agreement with Tolstoy's insistence that the Art that is accessible only to a privileged class is false, and with his belief in the innate ability of all men to respond to that true Art which, by uniting them in a community of feeling, helps to further the brotherhood of man. Tolstoy's belief that a writer "should stand on the level of the highest life-conception of his time" also corresponded to H. G. Wells' conception of the place of the writer in society.

Tolstoy's views on war and the part played by the "heroes" of history too were not altogether unfamiliar: his conception of obscure instinctive forces working among the masses of mankind was part of a whole reorientation in historical studies, in which many others including Carlyle (and in the novel, of course, Stendhal) had played a part. It is incidentally worth noting that Thomas Hardy was interested in this aspect of Tolstoy's thought: in 1893 he attended a lecture on Tolstoy given by Kropotkin, and in 1909 (June 28th) he wrote to *The Times* to express his general agreement with Tolstoy's "masterly general indictment of war as a modern principle", an agreement which perhaps found expression in *The Dynasts* (1904–1908). Indeed one might here venture the generalization that most of the serious writers after 1890 who dealt with war and its aftermath must at least have been aware of *War and Peace* (1869) as part of their imaginative heritage—though Stephen Crane (1871–1900) vigorously denied that *Red Badge of Courage* (1895), in spite of the similarity between the situation of his hero, caught up in a war whose origins and purposes he could not comprehend, and that of Tolstoy's peasant soldiers, owed anything to *War and Peace*. But at any rate Tolstoy's ironical portrayal of great leaders and generals—the Tsar nibbling a biscuit, Napoleon grumbling in his tent—was part of the general "debunking" movement in history, of which Lytton Strachey's *Eminent Victorians* was to be a later example. And at the same time Tolstoy's attacks on the multiplication of governmental institutions, on the growing power of the centralized state, on imperialistic ambitions, on personal luxury and indulgence, on idle and unproductive leisure, even his extreme theories on sexual abstinence all found an answering echo in various layers of English thought and feeling. And above all his onslaught on the evils of the new industrialism aroused a ready response among those whose peace of mind had long been over-shadowed by a consciousness of the "dark Satanic Mills".

It is obvious indeed that Tolstoy's teachings entered into currents of English thought that were already powerful, and from which, indeed, he himself derived nourishment. There is, for example, a marked similarity both in personality, and in method of attack, between Tolstoy and Carlyle. "Now, indeed, I am independent of the world's smile or frown, since I am in harmony with God, and have his smile as the light of my life. I have got into the blessed region of the 'Everlasting Yea'," Carlyle wrote, in terms reminiscent of Bunyan, but also not unlike those Tolstoy uses in *My Confession* (1880–1882). And Carlyle, like Tolstoy, insisted that human transformation must come from within, and that this process alone could renovate the external façades of institutions and manners.

There are obvious similarities too between Tolstoy and Ruskin. They range from a rough correspondence of views on Art—"the reign of Art," Ruskin wrote, "can never come until artists are workmen, and workmen artists"—to general agreement on the evils of modern industrial civilization, and the steps that must be taken to cure them. "Any system which does not recognize the principle of the Brotherhood of Man," Ruskin wrote, "is not political economy, but commercial economy, mercantile economy," and he asks "May not the manufacture of souls of a good quality be worthy our attention?"

There was a certain correspondence of outlook too between

Tolstoy and Matthew Arnold. For example, Ernest Crosby, who visited Yasnya Polyana in 1897, reported that Tolstoy spoke highly of Arnold, and we know that Tolstoy admired *Culture and Anarchy* (1869). There was also clearly a cross-fertilization of ideas between Tolstoy and contemporary American thinkers such as Henry George and William Lloyd Garrison.

But the most important aspect of Tolstoy's appeal to the English lay in the fact that he was perhaps the most powerful counterweight to the challenge of Science and Rationalism that the age had produced. In this respect his English admirers saw no inconsistency in Tolstoy's contemptuous dismissal of faith as the instrument of man's spiritual enlightenment—and his equally violent denunciation of the intellect. "All evil comes from the foolishness of reason, from the trickery of reason" Levin declares in *Anna Karenina*. It was this kind of reason, working outwards, that led to false ideas about progress and civilization, false economic theories, and the formation of institutions and governments. But there was another kind of reason, the kind which the child and the unspoilt peasant naturally possessed, which directed its light towards the secret of ideal harmony that lay within every man. And in this attitude of mind too, so strongly reminiscent of Rousseau and the Romantics, there was much to appeal to English traditions of thought and feeling.

It seemed to many, therefore, that Tolstoy had pushed back the challenges which had once appeared so inexorable, and had reasserted the claims of the older religious and philosophical ways of thought. For the sake of this much that was extravagant, alien, or uncomfortable could be forgiven.

It is hardly surprising therefore that much of Tolstoy's influence on the writers of the late nineteenth century and early years of the twentieth was on the more philosophical aspects of their work. It can be seen blending with that of other "witnesses of the age" (to use de Vogüé's phrase) such as Schopenhauer, Nietzsche and Ibsen—in the writings of William Morris, H. G. Wells and George Bernard Shaw, to quote three of the more obvious examples. But the important point as far as we are concerned is that even in fiction it is this kind of influence that is most common. Thus among the novelists we have already examined it is often possible to point to isolated passages which clearly echo some aspect or other of Tolstoy the teacher, but have little reference to Tolstoy the artist.

In Gissing's *The Crown of Life*, for example, the discussions on militarism and imperialism are obviously coloured by Tolstoyan ideas, and we know that Tolstoy was in the author's mind because at one point Irene enlists Piers' help in translating a passage from *War and Peace*. Piers, moreover, has a Russian friend, Korolevitch, who sells his estate and joins the Doukhobors. These instances, however, represent a mere surface depositing of ideas, and are not worked into the texture of the novel—though the ironical portraits of Lee Hannaford with his passion for explosives, and of Arnold Jackson, the ardent disciple of Cecil Rhodes, perhaps bear a slight resemblance to some of Tolstoy's symbolical types.

In that pastiche of literary influences *Evelyn Innes*, however, Tolstoyan themes are more closely integrated—though as we have seen George Moore consistently and perversely attacked Tolstoy the artist. Moore's description of Evelyn's growing awareness of the spiritual emptiness of her life is clearly influenced by Tolstoyan ideas. Thus Evelyn reflects how "the other night at dinner at the Savoy, she had looked round the table, at the men's faces", and had told herself that "she had not seen a man for years whose thoughts ranged above the gross pleasures of the moment, the pleasures of eating, of drinking, of lovemaking. . . ."

She visits her lover and he too and his whole milieu exhale the same atmosphere of futile luxury:

"Even his armchair seemed characteristic of him. With whatever hardships he might put up in the hunting field or the deer forest, he believed in the deepest armchair that upholstery could stuff when he came home. . . ."

And suddenly she sees all the comforts with which Owen surrounds himself, together with all his beautiful pictures and furnishings and objets d'art, as mere "attempts to capture Happiness". They reveal to her "the moral idea of which this man was but a symbol" and she is brought face to face with the realization that "life without a moral purpose is but a passing spectre, and that our immortality lies in our religious life".

And again Evelyn lies on her sofa and muses:

> "In her present attitude towards life nothing mattered except the present reality, the satisfaction of the moment; her present conception of life only counselled sacrifice of personal desires for the sake of larger desires. But these larger satisfactions did not differ in kind from the lesser, and all went the same way. . . . She asked, 'What do we live for?' and rose nervously from the sofa and stood still. . . ."

These passages echo the twists and turns of conscience which we find in many of Tolstoy's characters—in this instance perhaps it is Anna Karenina in particular who springs to mind. And the question which Evelyn asks herself "What do we live for?" and which underlies the whole book is the very core of the Tolstoyan challenge.

In its social aspects this challenge undoubtedly affected Galsworthy's choice of themes. His exposure, for example, of the gap separating the abstract principle of justice and its application through man-made institutions, recalls that of Tolstoy in *Resurrection* (1899). His treatment of labour relations and class cleavages, of property and privilege, of marriage and divorce, is like Tolstoy's designed to expose the hypocrisies, inadequacies and cruelties of the purely theoretical approach. His portrayal of upper-class life undoubtedly derives some of its bite from Tolstoy, and the ironical tone and purpose of his comments often resemble those of Tolstoy:

> "What indeed could be more delightful than this country house life . . ." he asks in *The Country House*. "Its perfect cleanliness, its busy leisure, its combination of fresh air and scented warmth, its complete intellectual repose, its essential and profound aloofness from suffering of any kind, and its soup—emblematically and above all its soup—made from the rich remains of pampered beasts?"

The tone is even fiercer, as we have seen, in *The Island Pharisees*. Here at times it reminds one, surprisingly, of Alexander

K

Herzen. The evenness and tautness of the style, suggestive of a bitterness and a passion only just held in check, the grim march from one revealing incident to another, the continuous beating on one note, are all curiously like Herzen's method of slow relentless exposure of the General and his way of life, for example, in *Who is to Blame?* (1847). It is hardly likely however that Galsworthy had read Herzen: the echoes have reached him by way of Tolstoy, who was undoubtedly influenced by Herzen, and indeed by a whole Russian tradition of social satire.

It was not only the destructive aspects of Tolstoy's thought, however, that attracted. One of the generalizations that can be safely made about his influence is that it gave a fresh impetus to "the novel of ideas" as a whole. It encouraged writers, like H. G. Wells, who set out to use the novel as a platform for a wide range of social, political and moral issues. It provided inspiration too for religious and philosophical novelists. Of these WILLIAM DEAN HOWELLS (1887–1920) is perhaps the most obvious example of the direct impact of Tolstoy's teachings, which affect many of the novels, from 1889 onwards. When in *A Hazard of New Fortunes* (1890), for example, Basil and Isabel March (the bridal pair of *Their Wedding Journey*, 1872) move to New York from Boston, they reflect on their new environment and on the evils of the existing social order, in terms that clearly derive from Tolstoy. When the heroine of *Annie Kilburn* (1888) after living for many years in Rome returns home she feels that

> "there is something in the air, the atmosphere, that won't allow you to live in the old way if you've got a grain of conscience or humanity. . . . It seems to me as if the world cannot go on as it has been doing. Even here in America, where I used to think we had the millennium because slavery was abolished, people have more liberty, but they seem just as far off as ever from justice."

In the same novel the Reverend Mr. Peck says: "Those who rise above the necessity of work for daily bread are in danger of losing their right relationship to other men". And the two Utopian novels, *A Traveller from Altruria* (1894) and *Through the Eye of a Needle* (1907), are permeated with Tolstoyan ideals:

in the imaginary land of Altruria, for example, all work is honour-
able, there are no servants, there is complete social equality, and
the inhabitants lead lives that are just, temperate and full of
loving-kindness. It is interesting to note too that in *The World of
Chance* (1893) Howells puts his finger on that element in the
American tradition which explains the appeal of Tolstoy's teachings when he makes old David Hughes declare his faith in "the
values of an earlier day, the values of Brook Farm, Emerson,
and Thoreau", which he feels "could still press themselves upon
the Christian mind" against a world that has "passed them by".

A proper appreciation of Tolstoy's great qualities as novelist
as distinct from teacher was slow in coming. The early reception
of the novels was by no means always cordial, in spite of Matthew
Arnold's advocacy. His Realism struck many contemporary
critics as "disagreeable", or "gloomy", or "lacking in reticence".
It was frequently associated with that of Zola : *Anna Karenina* was
included in the list of obscene books drawn up by the National
Vigilance Association : there was much in *Resurrection*, too, to
shock English susceptibilities. And his whole approach seemed
crude compared with that of Turgenev. As the *Athenaeum*
expressed it in 1887 in a review of Dupuy's *Masters of Russian
Literature*—"Tolstoy shows us the knife and allows us to dissect
his subject, whereas Tourguéneff's attitude is that of an artist."

It was the scale of Tolstoy's operations that at first repelled
or overawed the critics. Henry James and George Moore were not
the only ones to criticize him on this score. Andrew Lang wrote of
"a disconnected profusion, a crowding, a lack of proportion
which no impartial critic, however favourable, can overlook";
Julia Wedgwood deplored the "painful reproduction of what is
fragmentary and disproportionate"; George Saintsbury declared
"the novels are hardly works of art at all. It is, however, pleaded
for them that they are 'pieces of life', and so perhaps they are,
but in a strangely unlicked and unfinished condition"; and
Edmund Gosse complained that Tolstoy allowed us to see "the
stitches in the canvas". The size of Tolstoy's crowded panoramas,
indeed, continued to arouse a certain amount of uneasiness.
Though Mr. Percy Lubbock, for example, hailed Tolstoy in *The
Craft of Fiction* (1921) as "the supreme genius among novelists",
and agreed that the scope of *War and Peace* was adapted to its

creator's "giant imagination", he also felt that there was no real centre, and that in consequence "great masses" of material were wasted.

In the long run, however, it was generally accepted that the vastness of Tolstoy's canvases and the profusion of his materials were symptoms not of a lack of art, but of an extension of art. "Such an untidy book," Mr. E. M. Forster wrote of *War and Peace* in *Aspects of the Novel*, but as we read it, he asks, "do not great chords begin to sound behind us, and when we have finished does not every item, even the catalogue of strategies— lead to a larger existence than was possible at the time?"

There is no doubt in fact that Tolstoy's work had a far-reaching effect on the whole conception of fiction. The novel, until quite late in the nineteenth century, was regarded in some quarters as an inferior form of entertainment, not fit to rank with philosophy, or poetry, or history. But Tolstoy showed that it could contain all these elements, and on a scale hitherto un-dreamed of. Few critics before his advent would have imagined it possible that one day a serious writer such as Mr. Percy Lub-bock would be able to declare of any novel that it was "like an Iliad, the story of a certain man, and an Aeneid, the story of a nation, compressed into a book by a man who was Homer and Virgil by turns". For Tolstoy brought a new spaciousness, inclusiveness, and depth to the art of fiction, and it is a fair generalization that his influence, in some form or other, lies behind most of the ambitious projects of modern fiction, par-ticularly those that range far in Space and Time, that deploy vast swarms of people against vaster backgrounds—or that illuminate through the consciousness of a chosen group of individuals the impact of changing environments upon successive generations.

Yet this ability to convey a breath-taking sense of Space and Time represents only one half of Tolstoy's realistic method. Complementary to it is the equally powerful communication of the minute, the sudden blinding concentration of light upon some tiny detail of the vast canvas. It was a quality that seemed pecu-liarly characteristic, and we find many of Tolstoy's readers in the '80s and '90s—Anthony Hope and Sir George Trevelyan are examples—expressing amazement at his "intensity". It was a quality that took a good deal of getting used to, and some readers found it too painful—Burne-Jones for example declared: "I can't afford to read Tolstoy", and the earlier critics no doubt had much the same thing in mind when they spoke of Tolstoy's method as too "photographic", or too "microscopic". It struck some of Tolstoy's twentieth-century readers as an entirely new resource of Realism, particularly in its psychological manifestations. Thus Desmond MacCarthy believed that Tolstoy's use of the apparently irrelevant detail or thought sharply and unexpectedly focussed—Anna's sensation of diving, for example, as she throws herself in front of the train, and her sudden concern for her handbag—was by way of being a new discovery about human nature. "From then onwards," he wrote in *Notes on the Novel* (1932), "novelists began to try to get closer and closer to the actual content of the mind . . . and to surprise emotion at its source."

This was perhaps an exaggeration. The concretization of thought and emotion was hardly new to literature, and it is a quality that Tolstoy shared with the other Russian novelists. What was new in Tolstoy's case was the juxtaposition of the great and the small, the combination of extraordinarily exact observation with vast hinterlands and backgrounds, the giddy swooping transitions from one to the other that produce a sensation of sharp and sudden shrinkage. In this sense it is certainly fair to say that Tolstoy's experiments in the use of these rapidly shifting perspectives offered a new model of realistic technique which contributed to the evolution of the twentieth-century novel, and of which few modern novelists can have been unaware.

Nevertheless Howells was right when he refused to separate Tolstoy the writer and Tolstoy the thinker. "Axioms in philosophy," Keats had written, "are not axioms until they are proved upon our pulses." Tolstoy was certainly not immune to the "trickery of reason": it turned him at times into a tiresome and bigoted pedagogue, but his basic principles belonged fundamentally not to the intellect but to his emotional and imaginative experience, and it is from this source that not only the great novels but the best of the pedagogical tracts themselves derive their real force and conviction. For there the arguments and dogmatisms are fused with the rest of his experience and it is unrealistic to speak of them in isolation.

What is undeniable, however, is that the central element in Tolstoy's work had a particular relevance to the nineteenth century and its aftermath. For when all the theology and preaching are set aside the whole of it was related to one simple but devastating question: "Why Live?" As he says in *My Confession* (1884), all the problems with which he had vexed himself for years, "like lines converging all to one point", pressed relentlessly upon "one black spot . . . I had come to this, that I could no longer live . . . I saw only one thing—Death. Everything else was a lie." And indeed the whole of Tolstoy's work, both before and after his religious crisis, was in one form or another either a travelling towards or an exploration of this discovery. It is true that a coming to terms with the mystery of mortality is the one metaphysic which all artists in all periods have to absorb. It is true too that it is also a psychological problem whose resolution varies from one individual to another and the answers which Tolstoy offered belonged to his own personal salvation. But in a wider sense the question lay at the root of all the desperate seeking of the period, and much of the power of Tolstoy's influence in the West (its impact in Russia itself could, of course, call for a separate and specialized inquiry) lay in the fact that he focussed the underlying malaise of the age with greater force and intensity than any other writer.

Tolstoy's preoccupation with Death, moreover, related not only to the physical and spiritual fact but also to his vision of nineteenth-century society. Everything but the certainty of Death "was a lie", because so much of the life around him, he felt, was not life at all, but a death-in-life, and the average inhabitant of upper-class European society, it seemed to him, was, to borrow the title of one of the plays, little more than "a living corpse".

It was Tolstoy's pitiless exposure of the exhaustion and sterility of so much of contemporary society that caused GEORGE BERNARD SHAW (1856–1950) to hail him in the speech which he made at the Tolstoy Commemoration in 1921 as "the greatest social solvent" of the age, "revealing to us . . . the misery and absurdity of the idle-proud life for which we sacrifice our honour and the happiness of our neighbours". He knew, Shaw wrote in the preface to *Heartbreak House* (1920), that "Europe was stifling its soul", lapsing into "utter enervation and futilization" in the "overheated drawing room atmosphere" of the times.

The impact of Tolstoy's plays on Shaw and his contemporaries, indeed, seems to have been unaccountably neglected. Yet they aroused considerable interest among practising playwrights when they were first published and performed. It is interesting to note for example that Shaw in his lecture spoke of *The Fruits of Enlightenment* (1889) as "the first of the 'Heartbreak Houses' and the most blighting"—and pointed out moreover that it came "long before Granville Barker's 'Marrying of Anne Leete' or the plays of Tchekhov".

It was with Tolstoy's approach indeed that Shaw's real sympathies lay. *Heartbreak House* may have been inspired by Chekhov's "fascinating dramatic studies", but Shaw is careful to emphasize in his Preface that Tolstoy had "already shown us through it in his most contemptuous manner".

Chekhov's attitude, he explains, was that of the fatalist:

"He had no faith in those charming people extricating themselves. They would, he thought, be sold up and set adrift by the bailiffs; therefore he had no scruple in exploiting and even flattering their charm."

Tolstoy on the other hand

"was no pessimist: he was not disposed to leave the house standing if he could bring it down about the ears of its pretty and amiable voluptuaries, and he wielded the pickaxe with a will. He treated the case of the inmates as one of opium poisoning, to be dealt with by seizing the patients roughly and exercising them violently until they were broad awake."

One has only to recall the plays—pleasant and unpleasant—in which Shaw seizes his public by its shoulders and hustles it contemptuously through the corridors of whichever Heartbreak House or Horseback Hall he is exhibiting at the moment, to realize that it was with Tolstoy's shock-tactics that he sympathized rather than with Chekhov's *laissez-faire*. He too had no intention of leaving the house standing if he could pull it down about the ears of his inmates, and he too, in preface and play alike, wielded the pickaxe with a will.

Tolstoy's method, Shaw realized, was fundamentally a tragi-comic one. "Of all the dramatic poets," he declared in his lecture, "he has the most withering touch when he wants to destroy." Thus in *The Fruits of Enlightenment* Tolstoy "touches with his pen the drawing-room, the kitchen, the doormat in the entrance hall and the toilet tables upstairs. They wither like the garden of Klingsor at the sign of Parsifal." This "terrible but essentially comic method", Shaw felt, was that of nearly all the plays. Shaw's anger and the despair from which it sprang were not as terrible as Tolstoy's : nor was he capable of the merciless self-analysis and self-exposure to which Tolstoy subjected himself. But as far as dramatic technique was concerned Shaw too brought to the abuses and hypocrisies of contemporary society an approach that was "essentially comic", but in its undertones and implications never far removed from tragedy, and certainly left little room for thoughtless laughter or complacency. He too made ironical use of the trivial and the banal, he too employed sardonic anti-climaxes. It was his method too, in fact, to demonstrate the aimlessness and sterility of contemporary life by letting his touch fall upon "the drawing-room, the kitchen, the doormat in the entrance hall and the toilet tables upstairs"—indeed the long stage directions were often devoted to their exact and most dramatically effective placing—so that they too might be seen to wither, as at the sign of Parsifal.

These reflections on Tolstoy's plays are by no means irrelevant to our purpose, for the "withering touch" of which Shaw spoke was also the method of the novels. It was, for example, the prime cause of the shock produced by *The Kreutzer Sonata* (1889), for there it had fallen on the institution which above all others the Victorians held sacred—the institution of marriage. It was this stripping away of pretences and hypocrisies rather than any outspokenness of language or incident that upset Tolstoy's earlier readers. As D. H. Lawrence said of *Anna Karenina*, "the monster was social not phallic", and the point is admirably if unconsciously demonstrated by an article which Hannah Lynch wrote for the *Fortnightly Review* in 1900, in which she compared *The Kreutzer Sonata* and Zola's *Fécondité*. On the

whole, she says, she prefers Zola's "animal frankness" because
it deals with sex only, and not as Tolstoy does with marriage—
and marriage, she writes,

> "is one of those things in fiction about which it is agreed
> upon to be a little insincere. Whatever it may be in reality,
> it is necessary to make it appear an ideal state to the young,
> else how shall we persuade our young people to aspire to it?"

But the last thing Tolstoy would allow was that one might
be "a little insincere" about anything, and in the long run his
example, combined with that of other iconoclasts such as Ibsen
and Shaw himself, helped to break down old conventions and to
bring about a new frankness and realism in the treatment of
domestic themes. It is this aspect of Tolstoy's influence that is
important for example in Galsworthy's frank descriptions of
the married life of Soames and Irene, rather than the more
superficial resemblances of plot between the Soames-Irene-
Bosinney triangle in *The Forsyte Saga* and the corresponding
Karenin-Anna-Vronsky imbroglio in *Anna Karenina*. It did not,
it is true, always lead to particularly rewarding results: Arnold
Bennett's enthusiasm for "the superbly rendered domesticity"
of Pierre and Natasha in *War and Peace*, for example, inspired
some of his dreariest passages. At the same time Tolstoy's
satirical use of the trivial and the banal—the doormat in the
entrance hall and the toilet tables upstairs—in order to emphasize
the atmosphere of spiritual stagnation was not without its effect
upon such writers as Aldous Huxley and Sinclair Lewis. His
influence in this respect combined with that of Ibsen and later
with that of Saltykov's *The Golovlyov Family* (1876), translated
in 1916 (and compared by some critics to Galsworthy's *The
Forsyte Saga*), and also with that of *Oblomov* (1859), the famous
novel by Goncharov (1812–1891), which in spite of the truncated
nature of the first translation in 1915 soon contributed a new
idiom to the English language, and was a weighty influence on
Mr. Waldo Frank's *The Unwelcome Man* (1917) and on other
variants of the theme.

For Tolstoy's terrible question "But why live?" sounded
as ominously in the ears of the writers of the twentieth century

as it had in those of the nineteenth. He had probed it more thoroughly and illuminated it in all its ramifications more vividly than any other, and in this sense he can be seen as a powerful if indirect influence on all those who in one form or another set out to portray the sickness of contemporary society. For if this is fundamentally the question which challenges the social realists such as Galsworthy, Wells and Shaw, it is also at the centre of Mr. Aldous Huxley's exposure of intellectual and spiritual sterility, of D. H. Lawrence's plea for a return to "the dark gods", of James Joyce's evocations of cultural chaos, in fact of all the various "Waste Lands" of the period.

Its impact can be seen too, perhaps, in Virginia Woolf. The quality in Tolstoy that struck her most forcibly was his disconcerting ambivalence—the juxtaposition of intense sensuous enjoyment and an equally intense reaction of disgust. It was the conflict of emotions, she realized, that gave to Tolstoy's realism much of its hypnotic power and brilliancy. In Tolstoy's work, she says in "The Russian Point of View", there is always "an element of fear" which makes us wish to "escape from the gaze which Tolstoi fixes on us". Sometimes this is simply the feeling which Masha experiences so poignantly in *Family Happiness* (1886)—that "such happiness . . . is too intense to last". But this feeling is quickly followed by another—that "the very intensity of our pleasure is somehow questionable", and so once again we are forced, with Pozdnyschev in *The Kreutzer Sonata*, upon that inexorable question "But why live?" And there is always in Tolstoy, Virginia Woolf declares:

> "At the centre of all the brilliant and flashing petals of the flower this scorpion, 'Why live?' There is always at the centre of the book some Olenin or Pierre or Levin who . . . turns the world round between his fingers and never ceases to ask, even as he enjoys it, what is the meaning of it, and what should be our aims?"

It is an ambivalence of mood with which Virginia Woolf perhaps was particularly able to sympathize. Her own vitality and the intensity of her delight in the sensuous pleasures of the moment were related to an equally intense apprehension of the doubts and despairs lurking in the background of her consciousness. The scale of her spiritual explorations and of the backgrounds against which they take place is narrow compared to Tolstoy's, but in her novels too we find characters who sit at the centres of their respective worlds, so deceptively gay, and at the very moment when to all outward appearances they have achieved their most cherished desires, destroy the whole edifice of their happiness by their ceaseless questioning.

In *Anna Karenina* Levin is represented at one stage as the embodiment of human fulfilment, as opposed to the brilliant but sterile Vronsky. He has wife, children, domestic love, friends; he makes a success of the management of his estate; he neglects neither his social nor his religious obligations. But still the scorpion is there to destroy his peace of mind. Similarly in *To the Lighthouse*, Mrs. Ramsay, loved by all, is apparently happy in the midst of friends and family—but is still a prey to doubts and uncertainties. The question "Is human life this? Is human life that?" continues to mock her, as it mocks most of Virginia Woolf's characters. And for some indeed—for Rhoda in *The Waves*, for Mrs. Dalloway in her little room—the enigma proved too poignant.

CHAPTER NINE

GABORIAU WITH PSYCHOLOGICAL SAUCE?

FIRST REACTIONS TO DOSTOYEVSKY—EARLY EXAMPLES OF HIS INFLUENCE—CHANGES IN HIS REPUTATION

IT IS important to realize that Tolstoy's view of life, like that of Turgenev, continued to be part of the English cultural heritage, because the Russian influence is so often thought of exclusively in terms of the Dostoyevsky cult.

It helps to place Dostoyevsky (1821–1881) in his proper perspective, however, if we remember that 1912, the date of Constance Garnett's translation of *The Brothers Karamazov* (Russian publication 1880) and the beginning of the cult, was not really the starting-point of his reputation in England, but a half-way mark.

In the earlier period, there was in fact a marked reluctance to admit Dostoyevsky at all. In Germany translations began to appear as early as 1850, and most of the novels were known by 1890. In France too, practically the whole of his work had been translated by this date. No English translation, however, appeared until 1881, when a version of *The House of the Dead* (1861–2) under the title *Buried Alive* was published in New York. It was not until five years later, when Vizetelly published translations of *Crime and Punishment* (1866) and *The Insulted and Injured* (1861), that Dostoyevsky was introduced to the English public. Even then there were long gaps in between the various translations—between 1888 and 1894, for example, and then again between 1894 and 1912. The novels, moreover, were frequently out of print, and in 1903 Maurice Baring was informed by a publisher that there was no real market in England for Dostoyevsky.

Whereas, too, both in Germany and France there was, quite early on, a considerable amount of critical discussion of Dostoyevsky's work, in England there was no full-length article until

1885, and George Moore's introduction in 1894 to Lena Milman's translation of *Poor Folk* (which had been published in Russia in 1846) was the first full-length article wholly devoted to Dostoyevsky since 1889.

The welcome that Dostoyevsky did receive, moreover, was far less cordial than that accorded to either Turgenev or Tolstoy. It was attended by a certain air of patronage derived perhaps from de Vogüé, who, ranking him below his great contemporaries, described him as "le vrai Scythe", the most alien of all the Russians to Western tastes. Taking their cue from de Vogüé, however, English reviewers carefully distinguished between Dostoyevsky's Realism and that of Zola, as they had in the cases of Turgenev and Tolstoy, and again echoing de Vogüé, they praised his Christian message, his insistence on pity and charity, and his "religion of suffering". But a certain wrinkling of the nose on the score of subject matter and treatment is discernible in most of these reviews : even the titles of the novels, it seemed to one writer, were "somewhat repellent".

There was praise, some of it very enthusiastic, for Dostoyevsky's vivid characterization, and psychological power. But on the other hand his preoccupation with the morbid and the abnormal aroused some exasperation and a good deal of bewilderment. It did not issue, it was generally agreed, in the "enormities" of which Zola was capable ; it was, according to George Saintsbury, "not horrible or disgusting, but unattractive" —or to quote an American critic of 1887, "peculiar rather than nice". In its review of a translation *The Idiot* in the same year the *Spectator* was more outspoken :

"Authors desirous of popularity should bear in mind that the so-called realism which consists in a display of deformities, more or less hideous, dragged forth and paraded for the public to gloat over . . . is unquestionably unpleasant."

Although George Moore scornfully dismissed him as "Gaboriau with psychological sauce",[1] most critics allowed him extraordinary narrative power and intensity, even genius, in

[1] Emile Gaboriau (1835–1873) was one of the pioneers of the detective story.

single scenes, particularly in his "Dantesque" (a favourite adjective) evocations of poverty and wretchedness.

But it was almost universally agreed that he could not write a novel that even remotely approached a work of art. Thus Eugene Schuyler, one of the American pioneers in the popularizing of Russian fiction, in an article which he sent to the *Athenaeum* in 1875, deplored the fact that the "remarkable power of character analysis" and the "really great talent" exhibited in *A Raw Youth* (which was published in this year—so that Schuyler had presumably read it in the original) were vitiated because Dostoyevsky "allowed himself to give too much importance to episodes, to confuse the main subject and to draw out his reasoning to inordinate lengths". The 1887 review of *The Idiot* declared that the novel quite simply had no plot, and was "composed chiefly of scenes strung together on a slender thread of story". Similarly, a review of *Poor Folk* in 1894 scathingly dismissed it as "deficient in completeness of form", and "totally innocent of design or plot".

This was the translation for which George Moore wrote an Introduction, and a comment which he made on Dostoyevsky's novels many years later in *Avowals* (1919) succinctly sums up the basic difficulty which readers of his generation—and those who like Moore remained loyal to "the novelists' novelist"—experienced in accepting Dostoyevsky. "Before we can admire them," he wrote, "modern life must wring the Greek out of us. His farrago is wonderful but I am not won." The remark is particularly appropriate to the Aestheticism of the '90s, but the truth of the matter was that Dostoyevsky's fictional methods were utterly incomprehensible to those accustomed to the traditional forms of nineteenth-century English fiction.

But the inability to understand his methods was after all, in spite of the bouquets thrown to his "psychological power" and penetrating "analysis of character", symptomatic also of a complete inability to appreciate the levels of human behaviour and experience he was attempting to explore. What the average writer and critic of the nineteenth century meant by "psychology" was something simpler and more extrovert. The old traditions of fiction were still substantially intact, just as the economic, social, and spiritual foundations from which they sprang were still

substantially intact. At any rate up to 1912 (to take the date of
Constance Garnett's translation of *The Brothers Karamazov*
as an arbitrary dividing line) the consciousness of disintegration
was not sufficiently strong to establish the real significance of
Dostoyevsky's example. The average reader was genuinely
bewildered by his apparent incoherence, by the states of mind he
sought to convey, by his mystical vocabulary, by his preoccupation with disease and abnormality, by his negativism and "religion of suffering", because they were in direct contradiction
to the dynamic of his own society.

This is apparent indeed in nearly all the critical appraisals
of Dostoyevsky up to 1912. Even one of the most favourable
and percipient, the review of Dérély's *Le Crime et le Châtiment*
in the *Spectator* in 1886, which thought that Dostoyevsky had the
"most marked individuality" and was probably "the most
highly gifted" of all the Russians, and which showed more
understanding of his concern with "suffering and sacrifice"
than most, could see little prospect of Dostoyevsky's ever achieving popularity in England. All critics did not go as far as the one
who insisted that he was "totally incomprehensible to Western
tastes", but a reviewer of *The Idiot* in 1887 certainly spoke the
truth when he described Prince Myshkin as "very difficult for
the readers of the Western world to understand, so alien is he to
their ideals and desires". And perhaps the writer who, in the
Academy in 1903, set up Balzac as the antithesis of Dostoyevsky,
because he represented the natural aim of Western fiction "which
has been to express, either from the standpoint of hate or joy, the
pride of life", put his finger on the real crux.

As the period advanced, however, "the pride of life", and
the vitality and confidence that it implied, were subjected to
ever-increasing strains, and although the time was not yet ripe
for an appreciation of Dostoyevsky's methods and their significance, we can, especially as we move into the twentieth
century, see the signs of his eventual triumph gradually
accumulating.

To begin with, the later stages of the Idealist reaction against
the Rationalistic or Utilitarian philosophies of Darwin, Spencer,
Mill and Comte were marked by an increasing insistence on
the superiority of the intuition and the imagination over the

intellect, a revival of interest in mysticism and the supernatural, a reassertion of the individual as the centre of interest as opposed to the group or the class or the type, and a growing awareness of the fluidity of human personality. Schopenhauer and Nietzsche, Helmholtz, Wundt, von Hartmann and Bradley developed these new tendencies in the philosophical sphere, and helped to create an intellectual atmosphere more congenial to Dostoyevsky's ideas. As far as the more general reader was concerned, the appearance of such works as *The New Spirit* by Havelock Ellis (1890), and the introduction of foreign writers such as Ibsen and Baudelaire, also made it tolerably certain that the initial bewilderment aroused by Dostoyevsky's approach to human experience would soon be dispelled.

The gradual increase of interest in psychology helped the process. So too did the interest in Lombroso. His *Study of Genius* was translated in 1891; it cited Dostoyevsky as one of its outstanding instances, and dealt at some length with the seizures in *The Idiot* (1868) and *The Possessed* (1871–2) in order to establish a resemblance between the frenzy of epilepsy and the inspiration of genius. Although his theories were soon superseded they created something of a stir at the time, and as far as the general public was concerned they can be seen as preparing the way for the psycho-analysts, while they undoubtedly created a more tolerant attitude towards "abnormality", and its treatment in Dostoyevsky.

Other books too, by canalizing hitherto fugitive currents of thought and feeling, helped indirectly to prepare the way for the Dostoyevsky cult. Max Nordau's *Degeneration* for example, which was dedicated to Lombroso and which also praised Dostoyevsky, was translated in 1895. Its vision of Western society was certainly not calculated to inspire confidence or optimism and its standpoint could hardly be described as one that expressed "the pride of life". The description of Dostoyevsky, in an American review of Brückner's *Literary History of Russia*, as "the daemonic, mystic, ecstatic, visionary, satanic Dostoyevsky" suggests too that the mystique of the Dostoyevsky cult had already begun to form.

Some of the literary histories of the period, and notably Kropotkin's *Ideals and Realities of Russian Literature* (1905), showed little sympathy for Dostoyevsky, but on the other hand Maurice Baring's *Landmarks of Russian Literature* (1910)— although it approached Turgenev's great circumspection, was lavish in its praise of Tolstoy, and made the usual criticism that Dostoyevsky was "shapeless"—on the whole elevated him above both his contemporaries. Baring's enthusiastic praise of *The Brothers Karamazov*, which he had read in French, as "so great, so bountiful, so overflowing that it is impossible to find a parallel to it either in ancient or modern literature", helped to set the scene for Constance Garnett's translation two years later.

Even more important as a preparation for the Dostoyevsky cult was the work of Dmitri Merezhkovsky (1865–1941), who enjoyed a considerable vogue in the early years of the twentieth century. *The Death of the Gods* (1896), the first part of his trilogy *Christ and Antichrist*, was translated in 1901, and *Tolstoy as Man and Artist, with an Essay on Dostoevsky* (an abridgment of the first two sections of a larger work) appeared in the following year, and there were translations of other works in 1908 and 1909. Merezhkovsky's juxtapositions of Man-God, God-Man, and Christ, Anti-Christ, which were also woven into the stylized patterns of his novels, helped to provide the mystical vocabulary that was to be put to such energetic use a few years later.

In the first decade of the twentieth century, moreover, more tangible pointers to Dostoyevsky's future popularity began to appear. Laurence Irving's production at the Garrick in 1910 of a stage version of *Crime and Punishment* under the title *The Unwritten Law* provoked a good deal of interest—far more than Robert Buchanan's *The Sixth Commandment* had in the '90s— and there were other stage versions of *Crime and Punishment* in America. The Everyman edition of the novel appeared in the following years with an Introduction by Laurence Irving (it had been out of print for five years), and in the same year the Everyman Library also published *The House of the Dead*.

At the same time complaints of the lack of translations, or of the inadequacy of existing ones, and of the absence of proper critical guidance on the subject began to multiply. An article in an American periodical of 1900 for example blamed England and America for lagging behind Germany and France.

L

Finally it is significant that in spite of the equivocal and erratic nature of his reception by the critics and general public, even during this first phase he began to exert a direct literary influence. Even George Moore, for example, was not unaffected. Mike Fletcher has a suggestion of Raskolnikov in his make-up : there is a certain similarity of tone and atmosphere between *Poor Folk* and some of the stories of poverty in *The Untilled Field*. It seems likely too that the modifications of Zolaesque Realism in *Esther Waters* owed something to Dostoyevsky.

Rather more obvious were the Dostoyevskyan touches in some of Galsworthy's early work—though as we have seen in his case too the important Russian influence was Turgenev's. It seems clear though that he had read some of Dostoyevsky's novels in French —or possibly German. Certainly when he wrote *Villa Rubein*, which was published in 1900, he was already familiar with the idea of "the Russian Soul". In some of the earlier tales too there are occasional passages, usually connected with suffering or "the soul", obviously derived from him. In *The Prisoner* for example (1909) the narrator, describing his meeting in the German gaol with the convict serving a life-sentence says :

> "I felt then and ever since what they say the Russians feel—for all their lapses into savagery—the sacredness of suffering. I felt that we ought all of us to have bowed down before him ; that I, though I was free and righteous, was a charlatan, and a sinner in the face of that living crucifixion."

The language seems oddly strained and un-English for the year 1909—but it illustrates only too clearly the fatal ease with which the more superficial elements in Dostoyevsky lent themselves to imitation.

Although *The Brothers Karamazov* was little known by the general public before 1912 there are several instances of writers reading it in French or German translations. Arnold Bennett, for example, in 1910 explained in *The New Age* that he had read *The Brothers Karamazov* in French, and considered that it "contained some of the greatest scenes" he had "ever encountered in fiction", and that it was "one of the supreme marvels of the world". Like most of his contemporaries he criticized Dostoyevsky for his lack of Form—but it seems likely that he was one of the influences that encouraged him to break away temporarily from his French models, and that the formlessness of *Clayhanger* (1910) was to some extent the result of his example. Bennett also commented on Dostoyevsky's "grim humour"—in the scene of Catherine Ivanovna's bizarre funeral feast in *Crime and Punishment* for example—and there are places in *Clayhanger* where he seems to be striving after similar effects.

It was George Gissing who had first drawn attention to Dostoyevsky's humour in his book on Dickens, published in 1898. The passages where he compares Dostoyevsky and Dickens reveal an understanding of certain aspects of the Russian's work, and a depth of imaginative response to them, that are considerably in advance of his time. One of the major influences in Dostoyevsky's work was that of Dickens, and Gissing was the first to appreciate the basic similarities between the two writers. Dickens, he argued, but for the differences of race and upbringing, might well have written *Crime and Punishment* : the chapters dealing with Marmeledov's drunkenness and degradation were particularly Dickensian—and the elements of a plot involving murder, detection, a ruined girl who keeps her soul clean, a criminal redeemed by love, and faith in Christ, might well have appealed to Dickens.

What made Gissing important from the point of view of Dostoyevsky's future reputation however was his assertion that as a Realist Dostoyevsky was actually superior to Dickens— and his analysis of the fundamental reason. This, he argued, lay simply in the fact that Dostoyevsky was able to face facts which "Dickens was obliged to ignore or to hint, with sighing timidity". The character of Sonia, for example, was inconceivable in English fiction, and

> "the crucial chapter . . . the magnificent scene in which Raskolnikov makes confession to Sonia, is beyond Dickens as we know him ; it would not have been so but for the defects of education and the social prejudices which forbade his gifts to develop".

Raskolnikov too, Gissing argued—"his motives, his reasonings" —could not be comprehended by an Englishman of the middle class. As for the murder itself—Bill Sikes and Jonas Chuzzlewit

> "show but feebly after we have watched that lank student with the hatchet under his coat, stealing up the stairs; when we have seen him do his deed of blood, and heard the sound of that awful bell tinkling in the still chamber".

Gissing therefore re-stated the moral challenge as far as Dostoyevsky's Realism was concerned, while his own imaginative nerves stirred in response to the Russian's narrative powers. There can be no doubt that the example of Sonia in *Crime and Punishment*, reinforced by the strange circumstances of his own life, encouraged him to depict "fallen women" in such novels as *The Unclassed* (1884). As Morley Roberts suggested too, in his Preface to the 1927 edition of *Thyrza*, Gissing's sombre vision of poverty and slum life was clearly affected by his reading of Dostoyevsky.

It seems very probable too that in describing the more feverish states of mind of his heroes Gissing had the example of Raskolnikov in mind. Kingcote in *Isabella Clarendon*, for example, especially at the time of his illness, indulges in extremes of self-laceration that often strike one as decidedly "un-English" in the context of a nineteenth-century novel, as one of the other characters, Robert Asquith, seems to feel—"Something morbid about him, I suppose," he remarks to Isabella; "he looks in fact rather bloodless, like a man with a fixed idea."

Isabella Clarendon was published in 1886, and it seems likely that Dérély's *Le Crime et le Châtiment*, published two years previously, was among the translations of Russian books to which Gissing referred in the letter to his sister from which we have already quoted. But there was another writer who was even more powerfully affected by this translation.

Not long after the publication of *Dr. Jekyll and Mr. Hyde* also in 1886, John Addington Symonds wrote to ROBERT LOUIS STEVENSON, 1850–1894, criticizing the end of the book and suggesting that Dr. Jekyll instead of committing suicide should have given himself up to justice, thereby vindicating "the sense of human dignity". Other comments by Symonds make it clear that in offering his suggestion he was thinking of Raskolnikov's surrender to the police in *Crime and Punishment*.

His remarks brought an excited response 'from Stevenson.

> "Raskolnikoff is easily the greatest book I have read in ten years," he wrote. "I am glad you took to it. Many find it dull: Henry James could not finish it: all I can say is, it nearly finished me. It was like having an illness."

He goes on to express his enthusiastic admiration for Dostoyevsky's characterization, and above all for the "protoplasmic humanity of Raskolnikoff".

The vivid phrase is the most important in the whole letter, for it sums up as well as any of the later attempts the new conception of character that Dostoyevsky's practice implied. Stevenson in fact understood better than any of his contemporaries, better even than Gissing, what Dostoyevsky was doing, and what his example meant for the future of the Novel.

> "James did not care for it," he wrote to Symonds, "because the character of Raskolnikoff was not objective, and at that I divined a great gulf between us, and on further reflection the existence of a certain impotence in many minds of to-day, which prevents them from living *in* a book or a character, and keeps them standing afar off spectators of a puppet-show."

To writers such as James, Stevenson agreed, *Crime and Punishment* must seem "empty at the centre". As far as he himself was concerned, it was "a room of life" into which one might enter in order to be "tortured and purified".

The words suggest that Stevenson also understood, perhaps from personal exploration, the psychological bases of Dostoyevsky's concern with suffering, which were not to be generally appreciated until the advent of Freud and the psycho-analysts. At any rate in at least two of his stories he ventured into the Dostoyevskyan "room of life".

Dr. Jekyll and Mr. Hyde, has something of the intensity of atmosphere of *Crime and Punishment*, and Stevenson's interest in the theme of dual personality, though a far cry from the "proto-plasmic humanity" of Raskolnikov, must to some extent have been inspired by his reading of Dostoyevsky. But it is the short story *Markheim*, published in *Unwin's Christmas Annual* for 1885, which affords the most remarkable evidence of the way in which Dostoyevsky had stimulated his imagination, and which constitutes the most considerable example of Dostoyevsky's influence in the period up to 1912.

The story is in fact a miniature *Crime and Punishment*, and the parallels in incident, plot and atmosphere are very close. In both stories we have a poor student, not wholly wicked, but yielding to the promptings of his evil self, deciding on murder. The victim in both cases is a pawnbroker, a woman in *Crime and Punishment*, a man in *Markheim*. The gloom of Alena Ivanovna's flat is paralleled by that of the pawnbroker's shop—"Markheim had but just entered from the daylight streets, and his eyes had not yet grown familiar with the mingled shine and darkness. . . ." Raskolnikov experiences a momentary feeling of panic that his victim has guessed his purpose and has difficulty in hiding his confusion: Markheim has similar sus-picion and "turns his eyes aside". Both Alena Ivanovna and the pawnbroker at this point turn their backs on their visitors. Markheim's emotions as he realizes that the moment for action has come vividly recall those of Raskolnikov:

> "Markheim moved a little nearer, with one hand in the pocket of his great coat; he drew himself up and filled his lungs; at the same time many different emotions were depicted together on his face—terror, horror and resolve, fascination and physical repulsion, and through a haggard lift of his upper lip his teeth looked out . . ."

He strikes his victim down, and as in *Crime and Punishment* a pool of blood quickly forms on the floor. He is seized by "a weakness of the joints which he must instantly resist and con-quer", while Raskolnikov strives to overcome the trembling of his hands. Like Raskolnikov he takes a key from his victim and sets about unlocking drawers and coffers. And then, just as in *Crime and Punishment* Raskolnikov is disturbed by a visitor ringing at the door-bell, so Markheim is disturbed, first by the sound of boys running and shouting on the pavement outside, and then by a caller who bangs on the door of the shop with his stick. This caller, like Alena Ivanovna's, shouts "railleries" through the locked door as the murderer stands horror-stricken inside. And finally the pawnbroker's maid unexpectedly returns, as does Alena's sister Elizabeth in *Crime and Punishment*.

Markheim does not, however, strike again: in the interval between the murder and the maid's return is compressed the process of self-examination leading to repentance that in *Crime and Punishment* forms the real substance of the book. But the ending of Stevenson's story does meet the objection that Symonds had urged against *Dr. Jekyll and Mr. Hyde*, when Markheim vindicates "the sense of human dignity" by resigning himself to justice:

> "He confronted the maid upon the threshold with something like a smile.
> 'You had better go for the police,' said he, 'I have killed your master.'"

It is not only that *Markheim* bears a close resemblance in plot to *Crime and Punishment*: the technique which Stevenson uses to communicate his hero's feverish state of mind, and to build up the tension, particularly the sudden concentration on apparently trivial details and the effects of light, shade and sound, are clearly inspired by his reading of Dérély's *Le Crime et le Châtiment*.[1]

But at the same time there were limitations to both Stevenson's and Gissing's understanding. They shared the prejudice of the period against Dostoyevsky's Form. Stevenson for example, in spite of his impatience with Henry James' attitude in his letter to Symonds, described *The Insulted and Injured* (which he must also have read in Dérély's version) as "even more incoherent" than *Crime and Punishment*. Both of them, too, tended to over-

---

[1] A detailed comparison of passages in *Markheim* with the corresponding passages of Dérély's translation can be found in *A Russian Influence on Stevenson* by Edgar C. Knowlton, *Modern Philology*, Vol. XI, No. 8, pp. 449–454, December, 1916.

emphasize the aspects of Dostoyevsky's work to which they personally responded most readily. Thus Gissing's conception of Raskolnikov as "a man of brains maddened by hunger and the sight of others hungry", although it contains a truth, is by no means the whole truth. Similarly Stevenson's enthusiasm for *Crime and Punishment* as evinced in *Markheim* is focussed on the elements which are in fact the least important—the melodrama of the plot, and the production of macabre, spine-chilling effects. These were in fact the elements in Dostoyevsky which received almost universal praise, because they were so easily recognizable as belonging to the Romantic tradition; de Vogüé had touched on Dostoyevsky's affinities with Hoffmann, Tieck, Edgar Allen Poe, and Baudelaire, and many of the English and American reviews of Dostoyevsky's novels echoed him.

The characterization in both *Markheim* and *Dr. Jekyll and Mr. Hyde*, however, although it shows the "psychological realism" which most of the reviews of Dostoyevsky also singled out for praise, is, as far as facial expressions, gestures, and sensations are concerned, basically simple. *Dr. Jekyll and Mr. Hyde* is a straightforward example of the "*doppelgänger*" motif, and in many respects it belongs to the allegorical tradition of Bunyan's *Life and Death of Mr. Badman*. Stevenson in fact made no attempt himself to achieve the "protoplasmic humanity" which he so brilliantly diagnosed in Raskolnikov. Spiritual conflict is certainly present in *Markheim* but is dealt with perfunctorily and Stevenson's chief concern is with the narrative potentialities of the murder and the murderer's sensations.

In *Crime and Punishment*, however, these are subsidiary and Raskolnikov's state of mind is not a simple conflict between good and evil. His reveries on pride, free-will, the intellect, the rights of the "superior" individual, his subterranean spiritual journeyings towards his eventual salvation through grace, and the relation of these not only to Dostoyevsky's conception of Christianity and to his own psychological problems, but also to Russian religion and political philosophy—all the themes in fact that received their fullest expression in *The Brothers Karamazov*—had not yet come within the imaginative scope of nineteenth-century English readers, however gifted and however sympathetic.

The appearance of Constance Garnett's translation of *The Brothers Karamazov* in 1912 did not immediately put a stop to doubts and misgivings: *The Times Literary Supplement*, for example, still shook its head over Dostoyevsky's "prolixity, his endless digressions, his wild composition". A few years later Robert Lynd declared that George Moore was quite right in describing him as "Gaboriau with psychological sauce", that his characters were more like "madmen and wild beasts" than normal human beings, and that he was in every respect far inferior to Turgenev and Tolstoy. There was in fact always a hard core of resistance to Dostoyevsky and what he stood for, socially, spiritually, and aesthetically, with Henry James, John Galsworthy, Joseph Conrad, and D. H. Lawrence as its most powerful spokesmen.

But on the whole the translation was warmly received, and most of the reviews show that a process of adjustment was rapidly taking place. There was for example the important review in the *Spectator* which, as we have already seen, compares the Russian influence to a new Renaissance. It concentrates on the two factors that had hitherto proved the main obstacles to Dostoyevsky's popularity—his choice of "abnormal" characters and situations, and his "formlessness". It agrees that at first sight Dostoyevsky seems "so unfamiliar, so singular, so unexpected" that it is difficult not to be "repelled". It admits that his novels are "agitated, feverish, intense", that they "are screwed up above the normal pitch", that they "appear to be always trembling on the verge of insanity, and sometimes indeed to plunge over to the very middle of it". But it argues that Dostoyevsky deals with unusual themes "in order to assert, with a fuller courage, and a deeper confidence, the nobility and splendour of the human spirit". It agrees that the main object of the English novelists of the past with the exception of Emily Brontë (an exception that from now on was to be frequently made) had been to "treat life from the standpoint of common sense; to present it with sanity, with breadth, with humour; to throw over their vision of it the plain, clear light of day, and to stand on one side themselves with the detachment of amused and benevolent spectators". But like Robert Louis Stevenson it senses that this approach has become obsolete, and the most important part of the review is its recognition that in *The Brothers Kara-mazov* there is "an underlying spirit dominating the most hetero-geneous parts, and giving a vital, unexpected unity to the whole", so that what on a superficial view may appear "formless" has in fact the completeness of "some gigantic Gothic cathedral".

If there was a certain reserve in the reception of Constance Garnett's translation of *The Brothers Karamazov*, those that followed in rapid succession were greeted with almost universal acclaim, rapidly mounting to fervour. The remonstrances of a few intellectuals, Thomas Seccombe declared in 1916, were "less than futile. . . . We welcome the overwhelming flood." The majority of the intellectuals in fact handed themselves over unreservedly to it.

> "We heard on all sides," Mr. Frank Swinnerton wrote in *The Georgian Literary Scene*, "roars of ecstatic discovery. How pale Turgenev seemed! How material and common in grain our materialistic writers! How drab the life of the restrained feelings!"

It would hardly do now to describe Dostoyevsky as "Gaboriau with psychological sauce", or to dismiss *The Brothers Karamazov*, as de Vogüé had done, in half a dozen lines. At the same time the Dostoyevsky cult led to a great increase in translations from other Russian writers (though this was in part due to the unro-mantic fact that at this time they were free from copyright restrictions) and to a craze for all things Russian. Thus the hero of Mr. Somerset Maugham's *Ashenden* (1928) thinks back to those hectic days "when Europe discovered Russia . . . and Russian art seized upon Europe with the virulence of an epidemic of influenza. . ."

There is no doubt, therefore, that Constance Garnett's translation of *The Brothers Karamazov* touched off the Dosto-yevsky cult and the Russian fever. Excellent though her work was (and there have been criticisms from the linguists) it was not sufficient in itself to explain the extraordinary suddenness of the flare-up. Part of the reason lies in the fact that the various forces and tendencies, social, economic, philosophical and aesthetic, that we have seen gradually accumulating throughout the nineteenth century, had suddenly increased their pressure, and reached a point at which some event or other was bound, in Thomas Seccombe's phrase, to open the floodgates. In this sense the Dostoyevsky cult can indeed be seen in the light of a "renaissance": it symbolized a powerful liberation of emotions that had been held in check by nineteenth-century Rationalism, and by over-rigid aesthetic theories. Dostoyevsky, it was now felt, had revealed whole areas of spiritual and emotional life that had hitherto been ignored by the West. In addition the other influences of the period—Bergson, Freud, French Impressionism, Symbolist Poetry and many others, all making for the break-up of the old water-tight concepts of human consciousness and human behaviour, came to a head at about the same time, and gave to Dostoyevsky's novels an almost miraculous appearance of having concentrated into themselves the profoundest issues of the day.

The Dostoyevsky cult, however, can also be seen as the last flare-up of the Romantic decadence in response to a sudden acceleration of the self-destructive, disintegrating forces within contemporary society as the period of the First World War approached. The revolution in the concept of characterization, and the substitution of what Virginia Woolf called "this cloudy, yeasty, precious stuff, the soul", as the main centre of interest was in many respects an expression of the collapse of all firm values, and a symptom of devitalization. A subconscious apprehension of this fact, indeed, lay behind nineteenth-century suspicions of Dostoyevsky's choice of criminals, epileptics and simpletons as "heroes", and the frequent contrasts that were made between them and the vital traditions represented by the characters of Balzac or of the eighteenth-century English novelists.

But it was the war itself, coming so soon after the publication of *The Brothers Karamazov*, that threw all the various intellectual and emotional currents of the period into violent agitation, and turned enthusiasm for Dostoyevsky into hysteria. The most extravagant symptoms of the Dostoyevsky craze belong to the war years. Some of them, no doubt, sprang from the contortions which apologists for the alliance with the traditional bogey man of Europe were called upon to perform. Thus Miss Rebecca West in an article entitled "The New Barbarians" (the *New Republic*, 1915) told her readers that she had only to turn the pages of Dostoyevsky to be convinced that whatever sufferings the Russian people had endured at the hands of the autocracy had all "turned to sweetness, to a rapturous embrace of life, to a determination to clean the world before death comes . . ."

Of the same order were the books of Mr. Stephen Graham, particularly perhaps *The Way of Martha and the Way of Mary* (1916), with their rhapsodies on the passive "Dostoyevskyan" qualities of the Russian people which provoked the wrath of that far from passive Russian, Maxim Gorky.

At the same time, however, in the hectic atmosphere of the war, with its secret guilts and fears, the Dostoyevsky cult was also for many an emotional necessity. A balanced view of his personality, his ideas and his technique was no longer possible. He was, Thomas Seccombe declared triumphantly, "beatified, canonized, sainted": there was "something of Michel Angelo about his work, something of the major Hebraic prophets". Devotees turned to him for the vocabulary and symbolism of their own spiritual explorations.

> "I know," John Cowper Powys wrote in his *Autobiography* (1934), "that in certain subterranean motions of my spirit, I am much more like the Idiot of Dostoievsky than I am like Cagliostro. I dare say I have a touch of Ivan Karamazov in me too."

A review of 1916 declared that if the gospel of St. John were suddenly blotted out of human ken, the work of Dostoyevsky would replace it, and Mr. Middleton Murry's book on Dostoyevsky in the same year was to all intents and purposes an autobiographical account of its author's spiritual experiences in contact with the Russian prophet. In these circumstances it was not perhaps surprising that the Russian influence which had begun as an invigorating alternative to French Naturalism appeared, as it came to a head in the Dostoyevsky cult, to be degenerating into hysteria and mystical jargon.

CHAPTER TEN

ABSOLUTE REALISM

THAT the Dostoyevsky cult was in large measure the outcome
of hysteria is suggested by the event. For it died away almost
as quickly as it had come. In 1920, when *The Friend of the Family*
(1859), the last volume of Constance Garnett's translations of
the works of Dostoyevsky, appeared, it was already on the wane.
The end of the war had produced a general lowering of temperatures. The publication of books by members of his family,
of his own letters, and of commentaries on his work by Freud and
Adler, reduced the saint to very human proportions. The Russian
Revolution, though at first it enhanced his reputation, by virtue
of the apparent prophecies contained in *The Possessed*,[1] in the
long run militated against him, as disillusionment with the
Russian Soul, which Dostoyevsky himself had once proclaimed
as Europe's way of escape "from its anguish", but which was
now diverging dramatically from the lines laid down by Maurice
Baring, Mr. Stephen Graham, or Mr. Middleton Murry, grew
daily more complete.

As the cult became discredited, doubts as to Dostoyevsky's
value as a writer began to be expressed. Thus Edmund Gosse,
who in 1887 had been lavish in his praise of *Crime and Punishment*,
was in 1926 urging André Gide to wean himself from the influence
of Dostoyevsky.

> "We have all in turn," he wrote, "been subjected to the
> magic of this epileptic monster. But his genius has only led
> us astray, and I should say to any young writer of merit who
> appealed to me 'Read what you like, only don't waste your
> time reading Dostoevsky. He is the cocaine and morphia of
> modern literature.'"

[1] Or *The Devils*, as it is more correctly entitled in David Magarshack's
recent translation.

173

The reaction could not alter the fact, however, that a very large number of writers *had* spent their time reading Dostoyevsky —and the question remains whether Edmund Gosse was right in calling it time wasted.

It has to be admitted that a large part of his influence was of a purely transitory and worthless nature. The early examples had already shown how dangerously easy it was for the more obvious elements to be treated in isolation and he lent himself to this process far more readily than any of the other Russians, except perhaps Chekhov.

Unfortunately the vast majority of his imitators glibly reproduced one or other, or a random collection of Dostoyevskyan prototypes and stereotypes with only the vaguest approximation to Dostoyevsky's inner vision, or to his creative genius. There was, for example, what Abel Chevalley (in *Le Roman Anglais de Notre Temps*, 1921) described as the "flagrant opportunism" of HUGH WALPOLE (1884–1941) in *The Dark Forest* (1916), and its sequel *The Secret City* (1919). Both of these in addition to a good deal of debate on Russia, the Russian Soul, and the Russian Revolution, present us with a sado-masochistic, Stravrogin-cum-Svidrigaïlov character, called Semyonov. There are also, especially in *The Secret City* which is set in the St. Petersburg of Raskolnikov, with its menacing buildings and doorways, its furtive squalor and smoky atmosphere, numerous imitations of the more obvious Dostoyevskyan narrative devices. But indeed it is difficult to find a novel of Walpole's written during this period that is not, as Chevalley succinctly expresses it, "frotté de slavisme", and larded with Dostoyevskyan effects or pseudo-Dostoyevskyan mysticism.

There have of course been more original and more important examples of Dostoyevsky's influences. Here too however the tendency has been to isolate. An obvious compartment is that represented by Gissing's description of Raskolnikov as "a man of brain maddened by hunger". Thus although Theodore Dreiser's *An American Tragedy* (1925) and Mr. Richard Wright's *Native Son* (1940) undoubtedly sprang from the author's personal experience and observation, their treatment of poverty and crime also owed a good deal to Dostoyevsky, and particularly to *Crime and Punishment*.

Sometimes, too, it is almost possible to state the exact passage in Dostoyevsky which has provided the inspiration. Thus the famous description of the convicts in the bath-house in *The House of the Dead* which was frequently quoted in articles and books about Dostoyevsky has had a numerous progeny. A representative example is MR. LIAM O'FLAHERTY's description in *Two Years* (1930) of his visit to the Canadian Brewery Mission. It is what the nineteenth-century reviewers of *The House of the Dead* would have called a typically "Dantesque" scene:

"Are these my own, normal eyes, that see these men, distorted from the shapes and portraits of kindly beings into dark, rabid ghouls?", he asks, "Or has some ghoul made my own soul darker than the soul of a most brutal murderer, so that an epilepsy of my sight fashions darkness, sin and bestial ugliness on every face I see?

"And a cold sweat came from my pores with fear that I had descended into hell; such a hell as does encompass the mind of a madman."

The nightmare scene produces a typically Dostoyevskyan reaction:

"And then a counter exaltation raised me up, and I saw a beautiful purpose in this vision of human ugliness."

And finally comes the inevitable Dostoyevskyan genuflexion (though other influences are also in evidence):

"And I said almost aloud:

'Have you forgotten so soon? Henceforth this is your great curse as well as your great happiness, to see the souls of men naked, and even the most foul a brother to your soul, which contains it. Bow down, even like the simple peasant, who kisses the beautiful corn-giving earth. For the most criminal of them gives you a rich gift, the substance of beauty.'"

It would in fact be difficult to envisage any scene of this kind written after 1912 that would not contain echoes conscious or unconscious of Dostoyevsky's descriptions in *The House of the Dead*. The same bath-house scene for example obviously lies behind Mr. Stephen Graham's description of the horrors of the overcrowded ship in his book *With the Russian Pilgrims to Jerusalem* (1913), and in John Galsworthy's tale *The Dog it was that Died* (1919) we have only to encounter the words "In that camp of sorrow . . ." to know that the Dostoyevskyan formula of squalor-cum-Christian pity will inevitably follow.

It is the same with the treatment of the more feverish aspects of political intrigue. So many of the scenes and characters in *The Possessed* seemed prototypic that they inevitably, often unconsciously, affected writers who attempted to deal with the same material. Mr. Liam O'Flaherty again provides an admirable example with *The Informer* (1925) and there are times in Mr. Aldous Huxley's *Point Counter Point* (1928) when the world of Dostoyevsky's tormented revolutionaries seems to have strayed into Bloomsbury—Spandrell, for example, sadist and murderer, with a passion for Mozart, is in many respects a typically Dostoyevskyan character, a compound of Stavrogin, Svidrigaïlov and Raskolnikov. But indeed this aspect of Dostoyevsky's influence spreads far afield, and it is no exaggeration to say that it has been potent in many of the novels of our times that have dealt with mental or spiritual torment. James Joyce in *Portrait of the Artist as a Young Man* (1916) or Graham Greene in half a dozen novels, for example, were dealing with themes and situations that were urgent to their own particular experience and vision—but in the imaginative shaping of them could the example of Dostoyevsky be entirely ignored?

These are all examples of the way in which the influence of Dostoyevsky tends to resolve itself into a consideration of separate aspects. There is one novel, however, which brings together nearly all the elements we have so far discussed, and fuses them together with complete imaginative conviction—and which does so moreover quite deliberately. This is *Under Western Eyes*, Joseph Conrad's exercise in the Dostoyevskyan mode, which was in fact published a year before Constance Garnett's translation of *The Brothers Karamazov*. A consideration of *Under Western Eyes* must once again raise the question of Conrad's indebtedness to Dostoyevsky. As we have already seen, Turgenev meant a good deal more to him. There are, it is true, instances of "doubles" in Conrad—the balancing of Lord Jim and Gentleman Brown, or of Marlow and Kurtz in *The Heart of Darkness* perhaps

—and most brilliantly the subtle interpretation of character and motive in *The Secret Sharer* (one of the stories in *Twixt Land and Sea*, 1912). It is possible that Conrad learned something from Dostoyevsky here—but in actual fact his juxtapositions have little in common with Dostoyevsky's, and are much closer to the simpler patterning of the old Moralities. The realism of Conrad's tales can certainly take on a Dostoyevsky-like atmosphere of gloom and menace. But this is a dangerous game : if Emily Brontë had been living at the time of the Dostoyevsky cult she would no doubt have been dragged in by some critics as an example of his influence. Several of them did wistfully regard Thomas Hardy from this point of view, but in face of the evidence had to be content merely with discerning an "affinity".

Now the purpose of *Under Western Eyes* is a purely ironical, and even satirical, one. Conrad made this perfectly clear when he told Edward Garnett in a letter of 1908 that his intention was to "capture the soul of things Russian". And the narrator of the tale, the elderly English teacher of languages, stresses that he is a "mute witness of things Russian, unrolling their Eastern logic under Western eyes". It is through those eyes that everything is presented, and the "point of view", like that of Turgenev or Henry James, is absolutely integral to the story.

Often, indeed, the comment is quite explicit. Sometimes it is implicit, in a subtle exaggeration, half comic, half tragic, of the Dostoyevskyan Russian-ness of the scene, as when Razumov toys with the idea of confessing to Haldin that he has betrayed him :

". . . he embraced for a whole minute the delicious purpose of rushing to his lodgings and flinging himself on his knees by the side of the bed with the dark figure stretched on it to pour out a full confession in passionate words that would stir the whole being of that man to its innermost depths ; that would end in embraces and tears ; in an incredible fellowship of souls such as the world had never seen ! It was sublime !"

And sometimes the force of Conrad's own antipathy towards the Dostoyevskyan attitude breaks through and the irony becomes sarcasm :

M

"Razumov, who had beaten Ziemanitch, felt for him now a vague, remorseful tenderness."

The Dostoyevsky prototype passages are indeed brilliant re-creations of the spirit and often of the substance of the originals. There is for example the extraordinary scene when Razumov is interrogated by the General and the Chief of the Secret Police, which follows with uncanny penetration the essentials of the similar scene in *Crime and Punishment*—but without ever becoming a mere imitation. Here we have the same verbal fencing, the same cunning and dissimulation combined with the same wild desire to confess and to receive confession, and the same air of feverish unreality over the whole proceedings, as if everyone concerned was perfectly well aware of the truth all along, but was compelled by some inner necessity to go through the tortuous cat-and-mouse motions.

The evocations of darkness and misery in *Under Western Eyes* also reproduce the very essence of the Dostoyevskyan atmosphere. The apartment house where Razumov lives, for example, "an enormous slum, a hive of human vermin, a monumental abode of misery, towering on the verge of starvation and despair", is a replica of Raskolnikov's. Time after time too Conrad achieves that sharp-edged nightmare intensity, which is so characteristic of Dostoyevsky's realism. Razumov's hallucination when he is pondering his betrayal, for example, in which he imagines that he can see Haldin's body stretched out in the snow, reminds one forcibly of similar experiences of Raskolnikov.

And of course the confessions of Raskolnikov to Sonia and to the police are paralleled by those of Razumov to Nathalie Haldin and to Peter Ivanovitch and the assembled conspirators.

These passages constitute a brilliant *tour de force* : at times it is as if Conrad is demonstrating, almost contemptuously, how easily he can achieve the same effects. But this is not their main purpose : they are there because they too are part of the total ironic pattern. They are exercises of art, felt objectively not subjectively : behind them one can always sense the presence of the narrator. It would be incorrect therefore to cite them as examples of Dostoyevsky's influence, in the ordinary sense : the contrary is rather the case, for *Under Western Eyes* is what Conrad says it is, an *exposé* of the kind of Russian psychology that Dostoyevsky represented, and a vigorous assertion of a very different point of view.

This point of view, moreover, is quite un-Dostoyevskyan; Conrad's main concern is with the concrete human situations. Like the narrator in the story he sees Razumov not so much as a victim of his internal conflicts as of the external Russian world (as envisaged by Conrad) which has him at its mercy.

Nathalie too is the victim of this Russian world, and the secret hero of the story is the narrator himself, who is in love with her but powerless to save her from it. The essentials of the novel as novel in fact are typical Conrad—exile, loneliness, hopeless love and heroism, against a background of evil forces that overwhelm them. Conrad's rejection of the Dostoyevskyan atmosphere in fact is inherent and absolute: it is for him an evil presence and he uses it, like the "horror" in *The Heart of Darkness*, as a background against which the human drama takes place.

Much the same is true of the atmosphere of sordid intrigue in *The Secret Agent*. It is possible that Stevie is another example of the introduction of the Dostoyevskyan simpleton into English fiction or that something of Dostoyevsky's gloom has entered into the novel, but the real centre of interest is in Winnie Verloc's quite un-Dostoyevskyan reactions to the web of pointless intrigue in which she and the innocent Stevie have become entangled.

But what of the Dostoyevskyan "Soul" itself? The fact is that the closer we get to Dostoyevsky's innermost ways of thinking, the more false and strained do the attempts at imitation become. As Virginia Woolf said, the word "brother" sounds oddly on English lips, and if one detected a touch of strangeness about Kingcote in Gissing's *Isabel Clarendon*, one rubs one's eyes in amazement at some of the characters and situations to be found during the period of the Dostoyevsky cult. There is for example the old man in Galsworthy's *A Simple Tale* (1914) who washes the feet of his fellow inmates of the doss-house. There were too the numerous inspired simpletons such as Hugh Walpole's Harmer John (and perhaps Barrie's Peter Pan is related to the genre), the saint-like tramps whom we encounter in so many of the short stories of the period and many more examples that were, as Virginia Woolf declared, "nauseating in the extreme".

It is, however, the comments of D. H. LAWRENCE (1885–1930) that take one into the very heart of the problem of the influence of the Russian novelists. In his youth he was no more immune to their spell than the rest of his contemporaries.

> "They have meant an enormous amount to me," he told Catherine Carswell in a letter of December 2nd, 1916, "Turgenev, Tolstoi, Dostoievsky—mattered almost more than anything, and I thought them the greatest writers of all time."

The real key to Lawrence's reaction against them is to be found in the article he wrote, presumably during the 1920s, as an Introduction to his translation of Giovanni Verga's novel *Mastro-don Gesualdo* (though it was never actually used for that purpose). There he attacks the idea of "subjective consciousness", the elevation of the self-conscious ego, as a perversion of the true springs of "being", and as far as fiction is concerned he feels that "in this subjectively-intense every-man-his-own-hero business the Russians have carried us to the greatest lengths".

Similarly in his Introduction to *Cavalleria Rusticana* (1928) Lawrence insists that Verga's people "are always people in the purest sense of the word, they are not intellectual, but then neither was Hector nor Ulysses intellectual", and in the portrayal of his peasants and fisher-folk in this novel Verga is demonstrating the truth that it is not the self-conscious soul, the product of the intellect, but "the naïve and innocent core in a man" that is "always his vital core, and infinitely more important than his intellect or his reason". On the face of it there may appear to be a similarity here to Tolstoy. But what Tolstoy worshipped in the peasant was "poverty itself, and humility, and what Tolstoy perversely hated was instinctive pride or spontaneous passion". But the real antithesis of *Mastro-don Gesualdo*, Lawrence argued in his Introduction, was *The Brothers Karamazov*, and it was Dostoyevsky who aroused his fiercest anger.

> "I don't like Dostoievsky," he wrote to Lady Ottoline Morrell (summer 1915), "he is like the rat, slithering along in hate, in the shadows, and in order to belong to the light, professing love, all love. But his nose is sharp with hate, his

running is shadowy and rat-like, he is a will fixed and gripped like a trap. He is not nice."

For Lawrence saw in Dostoyevsky's famous Soul, in his professions of Christian love, pity, suffering, forbearance, and humility, manifestations of "subjective consciousness", an assertion of the will, and the self-conscious ego, far more extreme even than Tolstoy's.

"The whole point of Dostoievsky," he wrote to Mr. Middleton Murry (17th February, 1916), "lies in the fact of his fixed will that the individual ego, the achieved I, the conscious entity, shall be infinite, God-like, and absolved from all relation."

It will be seen that it was during the years 1915–1916 that Lawrence appears finally to have arrived at these conclusions about Dostoyevsky—the period that is when war hysteria and the Dostoyevsky cult were at their peak. They spring in part from a vigorous assertion of his own vitality, and the vitality of the real English tradition to which he felt so passionately attached, against the debilitating influences of the period. Obviously he had the devotees of the cult in mind when he wrote to Mr. Middleton Murry not long after the publication of his book on Dostoyevsky ". . . the trick is, when you draw somewhere near the 'brink of revelation' to dig your head in the sand like the disgusting ostrich, and see revelations there".

It was the force of his anger against Dostoyevsky and his devotees that led him perhaps to exaggerate (as it seems to us now) the importance of Rozanov (1856–1919). In his review of the translation of *Solitaria* (the *Calendar of Modern Letters*, July 1927) he confessed that at first he thought he had come across another "pup out of the Dostoievsky kennel". But he came to the conclusion that from Rozanov it was possible for the first time to obtain "what we have got from no Russian . . . a real positive view on life". For Rozanov, he felt, had shaken off the "virus" of European culture and returned to the inspiration of the real Russia, "the vast old pagan background, the phallic". . . .

Again in his review of the translation of *Fallen Leaves* (*Every-*

man, January 23rd, 1930) he sees Rozanov as struggling "to get back, to a positive self, a feeling self", a struggle which is expressed above all perhaps in his "harping on the beauty of procreation and fecundity".

It is easy to see that there was much in Rozanov with which Lawrence could find himself in sympathy. Indeed in the review of *Solitaria*[1] he declared "He is the first Russian, as far as I am concerned, who has ever said anything to me." But this declaration was also a contradiction of his admission to Catherine Carswell that there *had* been a time when the Russians "meant an enormous amount" to him. This praise of Rozanov in fact was an expression of his exasperation with Tolstoy and Dostoyevsky rather than of a serious intention to elevate him above them.

For whenever he wrote of Tolstoy and Dostoyevsky as *novelists* he was in no doubt at all as to their power. It was what seemed to him the abuse of that power that infuriated him. The "really quick Tolstoy", he declared in *Reflections on the Death of a Porcupine* (1924), produced great novels in spite of himself, and in spite of his wicked didactic purpose, so that even "the silly duplicity of 'Resurrection' could not entirely kill the novel". And in the Introduction to *Cavalleria Rusticana* he wrote :

"It was only as a moralist, and a personal being that Tolstoy was perverse. As a true artist he worshipped, as Verga did, every manifestation of pure, spontaneous, passionate life, life kindled to vividness. . . ."

In Dostoyevsky too he saw mixed with the "ugly perversity" an "amazing perspicacity". He was "an evil thinker"—but at the same time "a marvellous seer", and the Introduction to *The Grand Inquisitor* (1930)[2] which acknowledges the truth of much of Dostoyevsky's fable, to some extent modifies the earlier attacks.

To talk of "influence" in the ordinary sense of the word

[1] First Russian publication, 1912: *Fallen Leaves* was published the following year.
[2] A translation, by S. S. Koteliansky, of one of the most important episodes in *The Brothers Karamazov*.

would admittedly be ridiculous, though the attempt has been made—one of the reviews of *The Trespasser*, for example, suggested a close affinity with Dostoyevsky. But what is certain is that Lawrence's critical writings on the Russians take one into the very quick of his thinking. The issues they raised were the ones which most fundamentally concerned him. The Russians, in fact, were of considerable value to him because they provided him at a formative stage of his career with so much that was germane to his purpose, by way of testing out and rejection.

It is evident too that there is something in common between Lawrence's and Dostoyevsky's concepts of characterization. In a well-known letter (5th June, 1914) he warns Edward Garnett that in his work he "mustn't look . . . for the old stable *ego* of the character. There is another *ego*, according to whose action the individual is unrecognizable, and passes through, as it were, allotropic states. . . ."

Now it seemed to Lawrence, it is true, that Dostoyevsky's methods of characterization had nothing at all in common with this kind of exploration : his creation of symbolical types, his use of "doubles", his splitting up of the individual into various layers of consciousness, seemed to him merely a more hypocritically arrogant preoccupation with the self, "the old stable ego" narcissistically subdivided. Nevertheless the fact that Dostoyevsky's principal figures are, as André Gide pointed out, always in the course of formation, never quite emerging from the shadows, was closer to what Lawrence was attempting than anything that had gone before.

The question of Characterization of course involves that of Form, and Lawrence also had in common with Dostoyevsky a rejection of what he called the old "skin and grief form" of the self-conscious stylists and of those who shaped their novels round a preconceived *dramatis personae* of "stable" egos. In the introduction to *Cavalleria Rusticana* he wrote—"As a matter of fact we need more looseness. We need an apparent formlessness ; definite form is mechanical. We need more easy transitions from mood to mood and from deed to deed. . . ." It does seem likely in fact that in his treatment of Character and Form Lawrence at least benefited from the earlier example of Dostoyevsky. As *The Times Literary Supplement* pointed out in its article of

June 30th, 1930—"the transformation of the novel had already been accomplished by the time 'Aaron's Rod' was written".

And this indeed brings us to the crux of the matter as far as Dostoyevsky and the English Novel is concerned. It would be possible to multiply the instances of his influence that fall into well-defined compartments, or that illustrate the workings of the cult, but far more fruitful is the generalization that Dostoyevsky contributed powerfully to the processes which led to the emergence of a new type of fiction corresponding more closely to the complexity and fluidity of contemporary experience, and in this sense his influence can be said to have affected the majority of the serious novelists of our time. It is apparent, for example, at a comparatively obvious level, in the abandonment of the old Trollope-type family novel in preference for one which like *The Brothers Karamazov* used the various members of a family as symbols of conflicting ideals, appetites, and desires—as with the Gourlays of George Douglas Brown or the Gants of Mr. Thomas Wolfe. It is there, directly or indirectly and with varying degrees of integration, in Miss Dorothy Richardson's experiments with "the stream of consciousness", in the symbolical characters of T. F. Powys, in Mr. E. M. Forster's concern for the life that is taking place behind "the world of anger and telegrams", in James Joyce's surprising of Leopold Bloom's consciousness "at its source", or in Virginia Woolf's determination to get beyond the buttons, and the wrinkles and the warts, of Mrs. Brown.

.   .   .   .   .

It would be interesting, if space allowed, to examine the fortunes of all the other Russian writers. Some like Korolenko (1853–1921) were already known in the nineteenth century; others like Kuprin (1870–1938), Andreyev (1871–1919) and, as we have seen, Merezhkovksy, had won a following even before the appearance of *The Brothers Karamazov* touched off the Russian fever, while others like Artsybashev (1878–1927) and Bunin (1870–1953) owed their popularity to it. It was during this period too that the work of some of the writers of the older generation, and notably Saltykov (1826–1899), S. T. Aksakov

(1791–1859), Garshin (1855–1888), Goncharov, and even Gogol, for the first time attracted something like the attention they deserved. Each of these writers had his following, and each of them no doubt could be found to have created a little pocket of "influence". Aksakov, for example, whose *Memoirs of the Aksakov Family* (1856) was first translated as early as 1871, but who was not properly known until J. D. Duff published his translations in 1916 and 1917, had one particularly ardent admirer in W. H. Hudson—and this admiration undoubtedly helped to stimulate him in the writing of *Far Away and Long Ago* (1918).

The two writers who cannot be ignored of course are Chekhov (1860–1904) and Gorky (1868–1936). It is impossible to do anything like justice to them in the space of a few pages, but for the purposes of this inquiry—it is possible to consider them as glosses on or postscripts to the Dostoyevsky cult. Gorky is the most easily dealt with—as far as our subject is concerned. He was, it is true, quite well known in the first decade of the twentieth century, before Chekhov in fact; indeed Sir Compton Mackenzie in *Literature in My Time* declares that it was the success of the translations from Gorky in 1901–1902 that "first began to awaken in England a real curiosity about Russian literature". But much of this early interest was the product of anti-Russian feeling at the time of the Russo-Japanese War of 1905, and his real significance was not generally appreciated.

A suitable context for a consideration of Gorky is in his relation to Dostoyevsky. For he was often his direct antithesis. This is apparent above all perhaps in the contrasting attitudes of the two writers towards suffering. Whereas in Dostoyevsky pity is elevated into a religious principle, an end in itself, in Gorky it is a spur to anger, or action. In Gorky's *The Lower Depths* (1902), for example, Satin says: "We must *respect* man. Not pity him, not humiliate him with compassion, but *respect* him."

Dostoyevsky seemed to Gorky not only to represent the passive "Asiatic principle" in Russian life, but also to stand for a rejection of life itself, whose essence he believed consisted not in submission, but in struggle and creation. "Being and creating are one and the same thing," he declared in one of his essays.

"I see the meaning of life in creation," he wrote, "and creation is an end in itself and something that can afford us infinite satisfaction." It was for this reason that Gorky proclaimed the value and beauty of work, work of any kind provided it was an act of creation and pleasure. It is Gorky in fact who is the Russian with whom one would have imagined that D. H. Lawrence would have found himself most in sympathy (see for example Lawrence's poem *Work*). Gorky's name, however, seldom appears in Lawrence's writings, and this is indeed symptomatic of his reception in England. Of all the Russians perhaps he has been the least understood and the least appreciated. The Dostoyevsky cult was in fact too strong for Gorky's ideas and attitudes to be admitted. As Mr. Stephen Graham so aptly declared in 1916:

> "The Russia which Gorky attacks is just that which is spiritually interesting to us in England—the mystical and impractical Russia, Russia on pilgrimage, artistic Russia, and that which he wants Russia to be is just what would have least spiritual interest for us. . . ."

His influence in fiction therefore on the whole did not go much beyond the addition of a few details of squalor and brutality to the Dostoyevsky pattern Realism of the day ("an advance in grime" according to George Saintsbury). In Mr. Liam O'Flaherty's description of the doss-house for example there are suggestions of Gorky's *The Lower Depths* as well as of Dostoyevsky's *The House of the Dead*. More important, perhaps, was his creation of the tramp *genre*.

Gorky's own misfits represent only one phase in his development: they are symbols of a restless energy which has as yet found no satisfactory outlet, and are not therefore at all like the superfluous men of the Oblomov type; they lead directly on to the positive revolutionary heroes of the later stories and plays. The majority of the Western derivations on the other hand were misfits in the Bohemian sense, examples of rebelliousness for its own sake, or for the sake of self-dramatization. There is no doubt however that a large number of the adventurers and vagabonds of twentieth-century fiction, those of Mr. Hemingway, Mr. Steinbeck and Mr. Henry Miller for example, those of Mr.

Liam O'Flaherty in *Two Years* and W. H. Davies in *Autobiography of a Super-Tramp* (1908), possibly even D. H. Lawrence's hero in *Aaron's Rod* (1922), were all related to Ilya Lunyev, or Foma Gordeyev.

As for Chekhov (or Tchehov, according to Constance Garnett's system of transliteration), translations of his tales began to appear in the 1890s, and as early as 1909 Arnold Bennett was writing about him enthusiastically in the *New Age*. But it was Constance Garnett's translation of his works in thirteen volumes between 1916 and 1922 that really established his reputation.

He was brought to the public's attention in fact during the years when the Dostoyevsky cult was reaching, and then falling away from, its peak. And the Chekhov craze was in many ways a continuation of it. It was a continuation, however, in a minor key; it represented the first period of convalescence after the fever had burned itself out, a period of languor, melancholy and inertia.

The elements of a cult were certainly still present. But the religiosity that attended Chekhov did not demand as great an expenditure of nervous energy as that of Dostoyevsky—there was nothing to correspond in intensity to the religious and political excitements of *The Brothers Karamazov* or *The Possessed* for example, and the Chekhov *mystique* though as productive as that of Dostoyevsky in esoteric jargon and downright silliness, was more in tune with the mood of the times and the spiritual lassitude of the post-war era.

In actual fact Chekhov was neither resigned, nor pessimistic, nor "indifferent" in the sense that so many of his English devotees imagined. The whole point of his deliberate choice of the minor key, of his neutral colouring, of his banal characters and situations, of his apparent inconclusiveness was not only to reflect the sickness of the society to which he belonged—but also to demonstrate that even under such apparently hopeless conditions could still be found the symptoms, however unheroic, of human regeneration and survival. That Chekhov time and time again eschewed the bolt-holes offered by Dostoyevsky; that he attacked Tolstoy's *How Much Land Does a Man Need?* with the far from fatalistic cry—"But six feet is what a corpse needs, not a man. . . . A man does not need six feet of earth, or a farm, but the whole globe, all nature, where he can have room to display all the qualities of . . . his free spirit"—these facts were beside the point as far as the majority of the English intelligentzia were concerned.

There were exceptions of course—notably George Bernard Shaw who, as we have seen, perceived very clearly that the evocations of melancholy and futility in *The Cherry Orchard* (1904) held serious political and social implications. But the majority, failing to appreciate the fundamental realism and sanity of Chekhov's vision and purpose, handed themselves over to a cult which they had created more in their own likeness than in that of Chekhov himself. There are in consequence few examples in English drama which come as close as Shaw's *Heartbreak House* to Chekhov's underlying intention, though there are many, such as Mr. Tennesee Williams' *The Glass Menagerie* and Mr. N. C. Hunter's *A Day by the Sea* (1955), which continue to repeat the surface phenomena and the Chekhovian atmosphere. An examination of Chekhov's influence on the writing and practice of drama in the twentieth-century theatre would however demand a separate inquiry. As far as fiction is concerned, it is in the sphere of the Short Story that his influence was particularly potent, to a large extent replacing that of Maupassant.

Whether it was altogether a fortunate one is open to question. The skill of Chekhov in the choice and arrangement of his materials is in fact as subtle and as artistically complex as that of his forbear Turgenev. As Galsworthy pointed out, a tale by Chekhov only *appears* to have no head or tail, to be all middle like a tortoise; but unfortunately most of those who tried to imitate him "failed to realize that the heads and tails were only tucked in".

The influence achieved its best results, as always, where it ceased to be influence in the mechanical sense, and became a genuine correspondence of temperament and vision. Thus the elements in the Irish character which sprang from a pattern of social pressures and frustrations roughly similar to those in Russia and which had given a prompt welcome to Gogol and Turgenev, now found a good deal in common with Chekhov. There are for example more genuine Chekhovian elements in Synge's *The Playboy of the Western World* or in Mr. Sean O'Casey's *Juno and the Paycock* (1925) or in Mr. Denis Johnston's *The Moon in the Yellow River* (1931) than in all the more obvious Chekhovian concoctions of the English and American theatre put together. And many of the tales in James Joyce's *Dubliners* (1914), notably *The Dead*, are closer to Chekhov in tone, feeling and shape than the most painstaking English imitations.

One cannot help wondering in fact whether they are not really closer than the tales of KATHERINE MANSFIELD (1889–1923), who is usually cited as the most considerable and original of Chekhov's disciples. Of the reality of the influence, in a very straightforward sense, there can be no doubt at all. The evidence rests not only on the story *The Child-Who-Was-Tired* published in the *New Age* in 1910, which her recent biographer Anthony Alpers, somewhat generously, describes as a "free adaptation" of Chekhov's *Spat Khochetsia* (which had been translated as *Sleepyhead* in R. E. C. Long's *The Black Monk and other Tales* in 1903), but also on several other cases of rather obvious resemblance.

There were undoubtedly elements in her own temperament and sensibility that found a genuine stimulus in Chekhov. It came naturally to her to develop her stories by the gradual accumulation of impressionistic scenes, to use random details, casual incidents, unconscious gestures and remarks, making them suddenly responsible for the whole emotional content of a tale, as a small lever launches an unexpected weight, and to choose themes of melancholy, frustration, indifference.

In this sense Chekhov's influence acted mainly as a confirmation of personal preferences and a stimulus to their expression. When in *Prelude* Beryl cries out "Oh . . . I am so miserable—so frightfully miserable. I know I'm silly and spiteful and vain; I'm always acting a part. I'm never myself for a moment!" and wonders whether a more genuine self will ever break through the falsity—"Shall I ever be that Beryl for ever? Shall I? How can I?"—the emotional validity is not destroyed by the fact that we can also hear in the background the voice of Anna in *The Lady with the Toy Dog* or Nadyezhda in *The Duel*. And the same can be said when, at the end of *Bliss*, Beryl, who has overheard her husband declaring his love to another woman, contemplates the pear tree through the window and echoes the spirit of Gurov's musings above Oreanda Bay in *The Lady with the Toy Dog*.

" 'Oh what is going to happen now?' she cried. But the pear tree was as lovely as ever, as full of flowers and as still."

But with many of the tales one cannot help wondering whether the small charge of genuine emotion and observation that they contain is sufficient to justify the close similarities to Chekhov. When, for example, we read *The Daughters of the Late Colonel* we cannot help reflecting that these sisters too will never go to Moscow. Similarly when in *Mr. Reginald Peacock's Day* we read of the teacher who appears to his pupils as a strong and romantic figure, while his wife knows that in reality he leads a selfish, vain, and petty existence, how can we avoid thinking of the many similar situations in Chekhov—in *The Teacher of Literature* for example? For these cases and many more like them we cannot help feeling that the echoes are too insistent, the correspondences of theme, situation, tone, and treatment too pat.

And of course Katherine Mansfield does not possess Chekhov's comprehensive vision of the relation of man to his social background, and to the vaster backgrounds of Nature. She does not possess his fundamental sanity, or his objectivity, or his self-discipline. And though she learned a good deal from him it was certainly not from him that she derived the sentimentality, the parochialism, the coyness and preciosity which mar so much of her work.

Something more remains to be said, however, about Chekhov's part in the history of twentieth-century English fiction. When in 1903 Arnold Bennett reviewed R. E. C. Long's volume he wrote that Chekhov seemed to him "to have achieved absolute realism". And there is a sense in which Chekhov does mark the high-water mark of the Russian influence, and the final phase in the English exploration of the challenge of Realism. Chekhov's appeal did not depend solely upon the fact that he appeared to answer to the post-war mood and atmosphere. For there were elements in Chekhov's Realism as there had been in that of Turgenev—the restrained emotion, the discreet lyricism, the gentle pastel shades, the delicacy of form—that were in many respects more to the English taste than Tolstoy's giant landscapes in Space and Time and the overpowering, lurid colourings of Dostoyevsky. In many respects, therefore, Chekhov's influence was a continuation of that of Turgenev, and we have come full circle.

Apart from the devotees of the Chekhov *mystique*, there were serious writers who, though they might acknowledge the superiority of Tolstoy or Dostoyevsky, instinctively responded to Chekhov as they had once responded to Turgenev. If, for example, there is a Russian influence in Mr. E. M. Forster it is more likely to be that of Chekhov (or Turgenev via Chekhov) than of Tolstoy or Dostoyevsky. Indeed D. S. Mirsky argued (in the *Criterion*, October 1927) that Mrs. Moore's experience in the cave in *A Passage to India* (1924) when she feels she has been in touch with the Absolute, to find it neither tragic, nor noble, nor particularly awe-inspiring, corresponds to Chekhov's portrayal of a human destiny, in which the moments of regeneration are often unheroic, and the flashes of revelation often commonplace.

Much the same can be said of Virginia Woolf. She found it difficult to read Dostoyevsky a second time: she admired Tolstoy but she also feared him: and it was Turgenev, as we have seen, whose methods often corresponded most clearly to her own. At the time of writing "Modern Fiction" and "The Russian Point of View", however, she had not, as we have seen, realized this herself. But in dealing with Chekhov—who was in so many respects the heir of Turgenev—she was at her most eloquent. Many of her most penetrating remarks about the tasks of contemporary fiction are made with reference to his tales. Her doctrine that the modern novelist must realize that "Life is not a series of gig-lamps symmetrically arranged", but "a luminous halo, a semi-transparent envelope surrounding us from the beginning of consciousness to the end", is more apposite to Chekhov's approach than to that of either Tolstoy or Dostoyevsky.

At first sight, she pointed out in "The Russian Point of View", the tales of Chekhov seem oddly inconclusive—"On the other hand the method that at first seemed so casual, inconclusive, and occupied with trifles, now appears the result of an exquisitely original and fastidious taste", so that "as we read these little tales about nothing at all, the horizon widens; the soul gains an astonishing sense of freedom". And the effect which she describes here is that which she herself sought, both in her essays and in her novels.

In Chekhov's story *The House with the Mezzanine* the narrator finds one particular day from his past life returning most vividly to his memory "though nothing particular happened"—but in describing the small apparently random details that composed it—how Lyda stood by the balcony with a riding-whip in her hand, how fine she looked as she gave orders to a farm-hand, how she bustled through the house, opening one cupboard after another, how she did not come down to dinner until the soup was finished—he reconstructs the whole feeling and texture of the distant, inconclusive love affair. Similarly in *To the Lighthouse* (1927) we find William Bankes musing:

> "Are we attractive as a species? Not so very, he thought, looking at those rather untidy boys. His favourite, Cam, was in bed, he supposed. Foolish questions, vain questions, questions which one never asked if one was occupied. Is human life this? Is human life that? One never had time to think about it. But here he was asking himself that sort of question, because Mrs. Ramsay was giving orders to servants, and also because it had struck him, thinking how surprised Mrs. Ramsay was, that Carrie Manning should still exist, that friendships, even the best of them, are frail things."

Virginia Woolf's stories too in fact are built up round the trivialities of everyday life—sewing, tea-parties, picnics, random snatches of conversation, stray reflections—and their significance lies not in any formal dramatic story pattern, but as in Chekhov's tales, in the communication of the intangible shifting texture of human experience, and of the sense of mystery underlying it.

To sum up, therefore—as far as this particular phase of English Realism is concerned it can be said that the Russian Novel, as it reached the English through the work of translators, by providing an acceptable alternative to that of the French Naturalists, played an important part in the evolution of modern English fiction: and that of the individual Russian writers Tolstoy and Dostoyevsky made a profound impact, though it was Turgenev and Chekhov who appeared to many practising writers to constitute the quintessence of Russian Realism.

The English Novel, it is true, was no more dependent on foreign influences in the period with which we have been dealing than it is today. It has its own vigorous and deep-rooted traditions, romantic as well as realistic, and it needs no help from any outside stimulus. But its strength has always shown itself too in its extraordinary adaptability, in its powers of assimilating what it finds useful from a wide range of foreign cultures. The Russian influence, we have seen, has been called "something in the air, a layer of the atmosphere", and that description is applicable not only to transient enthusiasm, but also to the kind of influence that is the most pervasive and penetrating of all, because it has become part of the cultural climate and is therefore snuffed up as naturally as the air we breathe. The Russian influence may have been less than a Renaissance, but it was certainly more than a fever, and surely it is no exaggeration to say that the great Russian novelists, through the medium of translation, have become part of the English fictional tradition.

SUGGESTIONS FOR READING

The works of the English, American, and Russian novelists mentioned in this book constitute the obvious and most valuable suggestions for further reading. Translations of most of the great Russian writers are available in the *Everyman Library* (Dent) or in the *World's Classics* (O.U.P.). But attention is particularly drawn to the new and up-to-date translations now being issued in *The Penguin Classics*. The list offered below is not meant to be complete, but includes some of the books that are indispensable to a study of the subject. The particulars are of the English editions.

1. GENERAL

MAURICE BARING. *Landmarks in Russian Literature* (Methuen, 1910).
—— *An Outline of Russian Literature* (Williams and Norgate, Home University Library, 1914).

RICHARD HARE. *Russian Literature from Pushkin to the Present Day* (Home Study Books, Methuen, 1947).

P. A. KROPOTKIN. *Ideals and Realities in Russian Literature* (Duckworth, 1905).

JANKO LAVRIN. *From Pushkin to Mayakovsky: A Study in the Evolution of a Literature* (Sylvan Press, 1948).
—— *An Introduction to the Russian Novel* (Methuen, 1942).

D. S. MIRSKY. *A History of Russian Literature* (comprising *A History of Russian Literature* and *Contemporary Russian Literature*. Edited and abridged by Francis J. Whitfield. Routledge, 1949).

W. ROSE and J. ISAACS. *Contemporary Movements in European Literature* (Routledge, 1928).

ERNEST J. SIMMONS. *An Outline of Modern Russian Literature (1880–1940)* (Oxford University Press, 1943).

FRANK SWINNERTON. *The Georgian Literary Scene: a Panorama* (Hutchinson, 1950).

VIRGINIA WOOLF. *The Russian Point of View* and *Modern Fiction* (*The Common Reader*, first series. The Hogarth Press, 1925).

2. SOME IMPORTANT STUDIES AND BIOGRAPHIES OF RUSSIAN NOVELISTS

CHEKHOV

WILLIAM GERHARDI. *Anton Chekhov: A Critical Study* (Duckworth, 1928).

RONALD HINGLEY. *Chekhov: A Biographical and Critical Study* (Allen & Unwin, 1950).
DAVID MAGARSHACK. *Chekhov: a Life* (Faber, 1952).
—— *Chekhov the Dramatist* (Lehmann, 1952).

DOSTOYEVSKY

EDWARD HALLETT CARR. *Dostoevsky (1821–1881: a New Biography with a Preface by D. S. Mirsky* (Allen & Unwin, *1931*).
ANDRÉ GIDE. *Dostoevsky: with an Introduction by Arnold Bennett* Translated from the French (Dent, 1925).
JANKO LAVRIN. *Dostoevsky and his Creation: a Psycho-critical Study* (Collins, 1920).
J. MIDDLETON MURRY. *Fyodor Dostoevsky: a Critical Study* (Secker & Warburg, 1924).
JOHN COWPER POWYS. *Dostoievsky* (Lane, 1947).

GOGOL

JANKO LAVRIN. *Nikolai Gogol, 1809–1852: a Centenary Survey* (Macmillan, 1952).

GORKY

Whereas there is a fairly wide range of books about the other great Russian writers, including important studies published in the last few years, in the case of Gorky there is a dearth of up-to-date material in English. Gorky himself provides the best source of information about his formative years, in his three autobiographical books: *My Childhood, In the World* and *My Universities* (Translated by Isidor Schneider, and published in one volume, Elek Books, London, 1953). *Fragments from My Diary* should also be read. Note also FILIA HOLTZMAN. *The Young Maxim Gorky*, 1808–1902 (O.U.P., 1948), ALEXANDER KAUN. *Maxim Gorky and His Russia* (Cape, 1932).

PUSHKIN

D. S. MIRSKY. *Pushkin* (Routledge, 1926).

TOLSTOY

JANKO LAVRIN. *Tolstoy: an Approach* (Methuen, 1944).
AYLMER MAUDE. *The Life of Tolstoy: First Fifty Years* (Oxford University Press, World Classics, 1930).
ERNEST J. SIMMONS. *Leo Tolstoy* (Lehmann, 1949).
COUNTESS ALEXANDRA TOLSTOY. *A Life of My Father* (Translated from the Russian by Elizabeth Reynolds Hapgood) (Gollancz, 1954).

TURGENEV

EDWARD GARNETT. *Turgenev, a Study: with a Foreword by Joseph Conrad* (Collins, 1917).

J. A. T. LLOYD. *Ivan Turgenev* (Hale, 1943).

DAVID MAGARSHACK. *Turgenev: a Life* (Faber, 1954).

VIRGINIA WOOLF. *The Novels of Turgenev* (*The Captain's Deathbed and Other Essays*. Hogarth Press, 1950).

AVRAHM YARMOLINSKY. *Turgenev: the Man, his Art, and his Age* (Hodder & Stoughton, 1929).

3. SPECIALIST STUDIES

Among the studies dealing more specifically with literary relationships between Russia and the West, either generally or with reference to particular authors, I should especially like to mention the following, to which I myself am indebted, and which are recommended to the reader who wishes to study the subject further. Other specialist studies are mentioned in the text.

DOROTHY BREWSTER. *East West Passage: A study in Literary Relationships* (Allen & Unwin, 1954).

CLARENCE DECKER. *Victorian Comment on Russian Realism* (Publications of the Modern Language Association of America, June 1937).

ROYAL GETTMAN. *Turgenev in England and America* (University of Illinois Press, 1941).

CORNELIA PULSIFER KELLY. *The Early Development of Henry James* (University of Illinois Studies, Vol. XV, 1930).

HELEN MUCHNIC. *Dostoevsky's English Reputation (1881–1936)* (Smith College Studies in Modern Languages, Vol. XX, April–July, 1939).

ERNEST J. SIMMONS. *English Literature and Culture in Russia (1553–1840)* (Harvard University Press; Oxford University Press, 1935).

INDEX

199